CONTENTS

The Library–Classroom Partnership

Teaching Library Media Skills in Middle and Junior High Schools

Second Edition

Rosann Jweid and Margaret Rizzo

The Scarecrow Press, Inc.
Lanham, Md., & London
1998

SCARECROW PRESS, INC.

Published in the United States of America
by Scarecrow Press, Inc.
4720 Boston Way
Lanham, Maryland 20706

4 Pleydell Gardens
Kent CT20 2DN, England

British Library Cataloguing in Publication Information Available

Library of Congress Cataloging-in-Publication Data

Jweid, Rosann, 1933-
    The library-classroom partnership : teaching library media skills
in middle and junior high schools / Rosann Jweid and Margaret Rizzo.
   — 2nd ed.
      p. cm.
    Includes bibliographical references.
    ISBN 0-8108-3476-6 (pbk. : alk. paper)
     1. Junior high school libraries—Activity programs—United States.
2. Middle school libraries—Activity programs—United States.
3. Library orientation for junior high school students—United
States. 4. Library orientation for middle school students—United
States. 5. Instructional materials centers—United States—User
education. I. Rizzo, Margaret. II. Title.
Z675.S3J95 1998
025.5'678223—DC21
                                         98-21206
                                         CIP

PREFACE

Since the first publication of *The Library-Classroom Partnership*, several significant social, economic, and technological developments have affected the educational scene. Educators are discovering that there is a far greater number of "students at risk" fostering new programs in attempts to reach and educate these children. Economic conditions have caused serious spending reductions on the national, state, and local levels, at times resulting in staffing and program cuts. Technology has continued to explode with sophisticated hardware and dynamic software geared to use by students in all grade levels. Many of our readers have seen vast changes in school libraries — the on-line catalog replacing the traditional card catalog, and CD ROM and on-line services offering electronic access to reference materials. The reverse of these advancements is also apparent: school libraries have suffered budget and staffing cuts. The revised and expanded edition of *The Library-Classroom Partnership* deals with these issues, revamping the units, reorganizing the lessons, and including a new section on reading enrichment. Lessons that are no longer relevant have been deleted and others that meet the needs of today have been added. The electronic access of information is addressed but traditional printed sources are not ignored. The reality in school libraries is that there are never enough machines for all students and backup sources are needed when machines fail; therefore print materials are still necessary.

As in the earlier edition, the lessons included in this book stress the library media skills needed by individuals for lifelong learning. Long after adults have forgotten a particular fact of history or the techniques of balancing an equation, they will continue to use these skills in answering their questions about the world around them and to meet the demands of an ever-changing society. It has been well documented that the skills taught in a library are most effectively learned within the context of classroom work. To this end, the librarian and the teacher must form a working team to take each other's ideas and develop them into effective learning experiences for students.

The lessons included here are the results of such collaboration in two suburban schools in upstate New York. The units are built around the secondary library media and information skills syllabus, developed by the New York State Education Department. The lessons incorporate skills of location and use, skills of inquiry and investigation, and skills of reading enrichment. Covering the full spectrum of library learning, these guidelines are useful in any learning environment, school, or community.

The library media skills needed to successfully implement a library curriculum have been identified and the teaching of those skills has been incorporated with every discipline in the school. Students are made aware that research and reference are a vital part of the learning process, complementing and enriching every subject.

The eleven disciplines (English, mathematics, social studies, science, art, music, home and careers, technology, physical education, health, and foreign language) commonly taught in the junior high and middle schools are addressed in this work. Each lesson is a learning experience in the library skills and curricular areas. Each unit has been cooperatively developed using the expertise of the school library media specialist and the subject teacher.

The lessons are organized according to subject disciplines. Curricular areas that traditionally assign library research projects receive more emphasis but no discipline is ignored. The lessons are easily adapted to disciplines other than the one in which we have placed it.

Our goal is to give library media specialists and classroom teachers units that can be expanded, changed, and integrated into the library media program of their own schools. We hope that school library teachers and subject teachers will use these units to design a program that works for their students, teachers, curriculum, resources, and school facilities.

INTRODUCTION

Each unit included in this book has been streamlined to offer readers the necessary material to use the lesson as is. Some redundant features of the first edition have been eliminated to allow quicker access to information needed to teach the lesson. All pertinent components have been retained. Since most middle and junior high schools have at least some departmentalization, the units have been organized by subject matter and all feature the same presentation in each lesson.

Included in the units are:

Title: Description of unit

Integrated Subject: Curriculum area suggested for the unit

Assignment: Specific tasks to be performed by the student to reach the anticipated outcome of the unit

Library Media Skills: Continuum of skills needed by independent learners

Subject Curriculum Content: Lesson goals for subject area

Resources and Materials: Resource titles and other appropriate items used

Activities: Strategies used by the library teacher, the classroom teacher, and the student to complete the assignment

Electronic access of information is expected and encouraged but specific references have not been suggested since these resources are in a state of flux, with constant improvements and title changes.

Evaluation or assessment criteria have not been included in each lesson. It is suggested that the assessment routines of the subject teacher be followed. A variety of assessment approaches may be applied to each unit including checking off as completed, grading with traditional number or letter, rating on a scale or rubric, including in a portfolio to be assessed as part of student's growth over time, or conferencing with student.

In some units, additional suggestions to enrich or vary the lesson are included.

LIBRARY MEDIA SKILLS

Skills of Location and Use

- Learning proper library citizenship

- Locating and defining all sections of the library, including catalog, circulation desk, reference sections, and so on

- Discerning that all materials in the library are organized in a logical sequence

- Locating and using a variety of reference materials

- Demonstrating effective use of the library catalog by:
  * differentiating and understanding the information found in author, title, subject, and keyword searches
  * applying the information found
  * locating materials through use of the catalog

- Selecting appropriate resources by:
  * locating and using the table of contents of a book
  * locating and using book indexes
  * describing and identifying the uses of the table of contents and the index of a book
  * identifying and using glossaries, appendices, maps, and illustration lists

- Using periodical indexes in book and electronic form

- Using appropriate search strategies to garner information from electronic sources

Skills of Inquiry and Investigation

- Selecting and verifying a research topic

- Narrowing and broadening a topic when necessary

- Finding relative or alternative key words for the topic

- Using cross references in searching tools and references

- Finding specific sources of information

- Skim-reading to locate desired information

- Reading carefully to locate facts

- Selecting main thoughts and supporting details

- Extracting relevant information

- Synthesizing relevant information

- Taking notes

- Compiling a bibliography

- Preparing a report combining data from a number of sources

- Using a variety of report techniques such as video production, charts, computer, and so on

Skills of Reading Enrichment

- Developing discrimination in the choice of reading materials

- Forming methods of analysis and discussion

- Acquiring the habit of leisure reading as a lifetime activity

GENERAL

Unit: Orientation—Lesson #1

Assignment
Students complete activity packet.

Library Media Skills
- Learning basic procedures for using the library media center
- Learning the location of significant sites in the library media center

Subject Curriculum Content
- Learning a skill needed for research in all curriculum areas

Resources and Materials
- Library media center orientation booklet

Activities
1. The library teacher customizes the orientation booklet. The pages should be photocopied back-to-back and folded with the map in the center.
2. The library teacher welcomes new students to the library media center and distributes the orientation packet.
3. The library teacher leads the class in a discussion of "Old Favorites" and "New Technology," discussing each briefly.
   Answers to word puzzles:
   Old Favorites: books, videocassettes, magazines, microfilm
   New Technology: computerized card catalog, electronic encyclopedia, CD-ROM, laser disc
4. The library teacher discusses procedures for coming to the library media center and procedures for borrowing materials. Basic rules of using the library are presented.
5. The library teacher explains the general layout of the library and has the students place an "X" on the map to designate the place where they are sitting.
6. If the media center is using an automated circulation system, students are given their identification numbers.
7. The students work in teams to complete the map/matching list.
8. The library teacher corrects the maps as they are completed. Students should use any time remaining in the period to select and sign out a book or complete the matching test.

Welcome to the Library

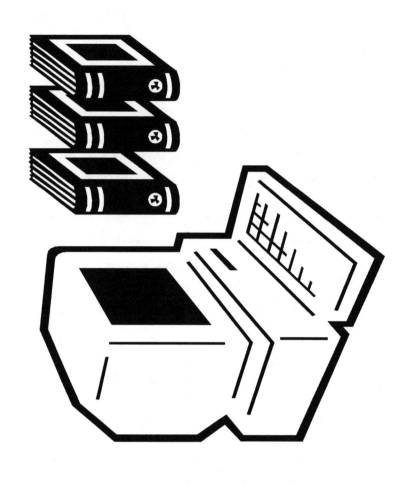

Please remember—

(Insert miscellaneous procedures and rules.)

THE LIBRARY PASS

(Insert a sample of a library pass along with the procedures for using it.)

LIBRARY STAFF

(Insert names of library staff members.)

LIBRARY HOURS

(Insert library hours.)

WHEN WILL YOU COME TO THE LIBRARY?

(Insert situations when students would come to the library, for example, with a class, from study hall.)

HOW ARE MATERIALS BORROWED?

(Insert procedure for borrowing materials.)

WHAT IS YOUR RESPONSIBILITY FOR
BORROWED MATERIALS?

(Insert statement of student responsibility
for borrowed materials.)

where you can find—

OLD FAVORITES—

B _ _ _ S

V _ _ _ O C _ _ _ _ T T _ _

M A _ _ _ _ N _ _

M _ C R _ _ _ _ _

AND NEW TECHNOLOGY—

C _ _ _ _ _ _ _ _ _ C _ _ _ C _ _ _ _ _ _

E L _ _ _ _ _ _ _ E N _ _ _ _ _ _ _

_ _ - R O M

L _ _ _ _ D _ _ _

DATE DUE

FIND YOUR WAY AROUND THE LIBR.

(Insert map and list of items to locate on

NAME

LIBRARY IDENTIFICATION NUMBER

Matching Test

Match the items in column B to the items in column A, and write the correct letters on the lines provided.

Column A   **Column B**

_____ 1. data disc inserted into the computer   a. compact

_____ 2. list of materials on a subject   b. modem

_____ 3. index of library holdings   c. biography

_____ 4. magazine   d. almanac

_____ 5. disc with high storage capacity   e. novel

_____ 6. book of maps   f. Internet

_____ 7. reference work published yearly   g. catalog

_____ 8. full-length fiction   h. microfiche

_____ 9. format for back issues of   i. *Encarta*
          newspapers and magazines
                                                   j. reference
_____ 10. reference work covering many topics
                                                   k. periodical
_____ 11. untrue story
                                                   l. encyclopedia
_____ 12. device for connecting to an
           on-line service   m. atlas

_____ 13. collection of networks   n. fiction

_____ 14. record of a person's life   o. bibliography

_____ 15. material referred to for   p. floppy
           specific information

Matching Test—Answers

Match the items in column B to the items in column A, and write
the correct letters on the lines provided.

Column A	Column B
__p__ 1. data disc inserted into the computer	a. compact
__o__ 2. list of materials on a subject	b. modem
__q__ 3. index of library holdings	c. biography
__k__ 4. magazine	d. almanac
__a__ 5. disc with high storage capacity	e. novel
__m__ 6. book of maps	f. Internet
__d__ 7. reference work published yearly	g. catalog
__e__ 8. full-length fiction	h. microfiche
__h__ 9. format for back issues of newspapers and magazines	i. *Encarta*
__l__ 10. reference work covering many topics	j. reference
__n__ 11. untrue story	k. periodical
__b__ 12. device for connecting to an on-line service	l. encyclopedia
__f__ 13. collection of networks	m. atlas
__c__ 14. record of a person's life	n. fiction
__j__ 15. material referred to for specific information	o. bibliography
	p. floppy

9

Unit: Orientation—Lesson #2

Assignment
Students complete activity sheet.

Library Media Skills
- Understanding the different types of searches to be done in a catalog
- Using the card catalog or automated catalog to do author, title, and subject searches
- Locating materials
- Learning about the different types of periodicals subscribed to by the media center and supplying titles for various subject categories
- Reviewing or learning to use audiovisual equipment and computers

Subject Curriculum Content
- Learning a skill needed for research in all curriculum areas

Resources and Materials
- Numbered envelope containing cards for author, title, and subject searches and shelf marker
- Worksheet

Activities
1. The library teacher prepares the envelopes for individual students. Names of authors, titles, and subjects taken from the automated or card catalog are written on separate index cards. Strips of oaktag are cut. Small manila envelopes are numbered. One author, one title, and one author card, along with a strip of oaktag are each numbered according to the envelope in which they will be placed.
2. The library teacher distributes an envelope and a worksheet to each student instructing the students to write their envelope numbers on their worksheets in case they do not finish during the class period.
3. The library teacher explains the cataloging system used in the library and points out that students must complete question #1 before they can do question #2 and, in order to use the shelf marker effectively, must find and bring the books for initialing one at a time.
4. The library teacher briefly explains the variety of periodicals the library subscribes to.
5. The library teacher demonstrates the operations of whatever pieces of audiovisual equipment the students will be asked to work with.
6. It is helpful to divide the students so that some begin with question #1 and then do question #2, and others begin with question #3.
7. The library teacher and classroom teacher circulate to assist students and correct or initial questions as they are completed.

I. In your envelope, there are three cards. You will be using them to answer questions using the library catalog.

   A. On the <u>first card,</u> there is the name of an author. Type in the name and answer the following questions:

   Author_____

   Book title_____

   Publisher_____

   Call number_____

   B. On the <u>second card,</u> there is a title. Type in the title and answer the following questions:

   Title_____

   Author of the book_____

   Publisher_____

   Call number_____

   C. On the <u>third card,</u> there is a subject. Type in the subject and answer the following questions:

   Subject_____

   Number of books on the subject_____

   Call number(s)_____

   Title of one book _____

   Author of that book_____

   Call number of that book_____

II. Locate each of the books, one at a time. Mark the space on the shelf with your marker. Bring the books to your teacher or the librarian for initialing.

IA. _____ IB. _____ IC. _____

III. **Name one magazine in each category that this library subscribes to.**

       A. Weekly news magazine _____

       B. Sports magazine _____

       C. Geography/travel magazine _____

IV. **Show that you can start up each of the following pieces of equipment. Either a librarian or a teacher will initial this answer sheet on the blank line to show that you are able to work with the machine.**

       A. Microfiche reader _____

       B. Computer _____

Unit: Orientation—Lesson #3

Assignment

Students find materials on a given subject in a variety of sources and complete a worksheet.

Library Media Skills
- Locating information on a given subject in a variety of sources
- Using the library catalog
- Using encyclopedias
- Using magazine indexes, in book and compact disc formats
- Using the pamphlet file
- Synthesizing facts from a variety of sources

Subject Curriculum Content
- Learning a skill needed for research in all curriculum areas

Resources and Materials
- Cards on which subjects have been written
- Worksheet
- Encyclopedias, in book and compact disc formats
- Magazine indexes, in book and compact disc formats
- Pamphlet file

Activities
1. The library teacher locates topics that could be found in the catalog, encyclopedias, magazine indexes, and the pamphlet file. These are written on individual index cards and placed in a fishbowl.
2. The library teacher distributes a worksheet to each student. Each student then selects a topic card from the fishbowl and writes the topic on the worksheet.
3. The library teacher instructs students on the use of magazine indexes and the pamphlet file.
4. The library teacher and the classroom teacher circulate to assist students and correct the questions as they are completed.

NAME_____ PERIOD_____

DATE_____ **ORIENTATION—LESSON #3**

TOPIC_____

Computer or card catalog--Look up a book on your topic, and provide the following information:

      Title_____

      Author_____ Call number_____

      One fact about your topic_____

Encyclopedia--Look your topic in an encyclopedia, and provide the following information:

      Title of encyclopedia_____

      Format (book or compact disc)_____

      One fact about your topic_____

Magazine index--Locate your subject in a magazine index, and provide the following information about the entry:

      Name of magazine index_____

      Format (book or compact disc)_____

      Title of article_____

      Title of magazine_____ Date_____

      One fact about your topic_____

Pamphlet file--Locate the file on your subject, and provide the following information:

      Title of pamphlet or other material_____

      One fact about your topic_____

Unit: Orientation—Lesson #4

Assignment

The students circulate among Dewey stations and complete questions on the worksheet.

Library Media Skills

- Learning to use reference materials from different Dewey categories
- Synthesizing information

Subject Curriculum Content

- Learning a skill needed for research in all curriculum areas

Resources and Materials

- Reference materials from different Dewey categories
- Worksheet

Activities

1. The library teacher selects reference materials from different Dewey categories striving to include those that are intriguing, overlooked, and useful.
2. The library teacher creates "stations" of specific Dewey categories and labels them.
3. The library teacher distributes the worksheet, explains the layout of the stations, and divides the students so they begin at different locations.
4. The library teacher and the classroom teacher circulate to assist students and correct answers as they are completed.

NAME_____ PERIOD_____

DATE_____ **ORIENTATION—LESSON #4**

At each station, use the indicated reference materials to find the answers to the questions.

Station #1--Ref\000-Ref\499

Famous First Facts

Who made the first balloon flight?_____

When?_____

What was remarkable about him?_____

Larousse World Mythology

Who was Bragi in German mythology?_____

The American Book of Days

What happened on December 16?_____

Roget's II The New Thesaurus

What are three synonyms for the verb cut?_____

Station #2--Ref\500-Ref\599

Compton's Illustrated Science Dictionary

What is a tsunami?_____

The Dorling Kindersley Science Encyclopedia

What is a zeugen?_____

What causes them to form?_____

Encyclopedia of the Animal World

Describe the shrew._____

How many species are in the same class as the shrew?_____

In what areas are they NOT found?_____

A Natural History of American Birds

Describe the song of the catbird._____

Station #3--Ref\600-Ref\699

Scientists and Inventors

What did Christopher Latham Sholes invent?_____

The Epic of Flight: The Giant Airships

When and where did the *Hindenburg* crash?_____

The Ship

What is special about the clipper ship *Rainbow*?_____

When and where was it launched?_____

Station #4--Ref\700-Ref\799

The Golden Encyclopedia of Music

What is a lute?_____

Where and when was it used?_____

The Movies

What was Rin-Tin-Tin?_____

What was one movie in which he starred?_____

The Arts in America: The Colonial Period

What craft did Paul Revere work at?_____

Station #5--Ref\800-Ref\899

Brewer's Dictionary of Phrase and Fable

How many knights met at the Round Table?_____

Oxford Companion to American Literature

When was *Huckleberry Finn* published?_____

Twentieth Century Children's Writers

Where does Judy Blume live?_____

Authors and Artists for Young Adults

Where was Lois Lowry born?_____

Fifth Book of Junior Authors and Illustrators

Where did Norma Fox Mazer grow up?_____

Station #6--Ref\920

People Who Made America

What kind of business was John D. Rockefeller in?_____

Facts about the Presidents

What college did Thomas Jefferson attend?_____

Webster's Biographical Dictionary

What ancient remains were studied by Sir Flinders Petrie?

_____

Webster's American Biographies

For how long did Thomas Jefferson receive formal schooling?

_____

Concise Dictionary of American Biography

Besides being an inventor and engineer, what else did

Robert Fulton do?_____

Station #7--Ref\900-Ref\919.9 and Ref\922-Ref\999

This Fabulous Century, 1950-1960

How long did it take for "I Love Lucy" to become TV's most

popular show in the early 1950s?_____

Webster's Geographical Dictionary

In what country is Oulu?_____

The Civil War: Brother against Brother

When was Jefferson Davis sworn in as President of the

Confederate States?_____

Concise Dictionary of American History

What president was responsible for the Good Neighbor

Policy?_____

The Oxford History of the Classical World

What was based on the Roman Twelve Tables?_____

Orientation—Lesson #4
Answer Key

Station #1--Ref\000-Ref\499
- *Famous First Facts*: Edward Warren; June 24, 1784; he was 13 years old.
- *Larousse World Mythology*: god of poetry
- *The American Book of Days*: Boston Tea Party
- *Roget's II The New Thesaurus*: gash, incise, pierce, slash, slit

Station #2--Ref\500-Ref\599
- *Compton's Illustrated Science Dictionary*: a giant wave caused by an earthquake or a volcanic eruption on the ocean floor
- *The Dorling Kindersley Science Encyclopedia*: a top-heavy rock structure; exposed rocks are sandblasted into unusual shapes and polished by erosion, which happens when sand is flung about by the wind.
- *Encyclopedia of the Animal World*: small mouselike mammal with short legs, long pointed nose, and long tail; over 200; polar regions, Australia, New Zealand, South America
- *A Natural History of American Birds*: medley of short phrases often interrupted by harsh "mewing" note

Station #3--Ref\600-Ref\699
- *Scientists and Inventors*: typewriter
- *The Epic of Flight: The Giant Airships*: Lakehurst, New Jersey, on May 6, 1937
- *The Ship*: considered to be the first clipper; New York in 1845

Station #4--Ref\700-Ref\799
- *The Golden Encyclopedia of Music*: long-necked stringed instrument played by plucking; Western Europe in 16th and 17th centuries
- *The Movies*: a dog; "Rinty of the Desert"
- *The Arts in America: The Colonial Period*: silversmith

Station #5--Ref\800-Ref\899

- *Brewer's Dictionary of Phrase and Fable*: 150
- *Oxford Companion to American Literature*: 1884
- *Twentieth Century Children's Writers*: New Mexico and New York City
- *Authors and Artists for Young Adults*: Honolulu
- *Fifth Book of Junior Authors and Illustrators*: Glens Falls, New York

Station #6--Ref\920

- *People Who Made America*: oil
- *Facts about the Presidents*: College of William and Mary
- *Webster's Biographical Dictionary*: Stonehenge
- *Webster's American Biographies*: 3 months
- *Concise Dictionary of American Biography*: artist

Station #7--Ref\900-Ref\919.9 and Ref\922-Ref\999

- *This Fabulous Century, 1950-1960*: 6 months
- *Webster's Geographical Dictionary*: Finland
- *The Civil War: Brother against Brother*: February 18, 1861
- *Concise Dictionary of American History*: Franklin Delano Roosevelt
- *The Oxford History of the Classical World*: Roman civil law in age of Cicero

Unit: Orientation—Lesson #5

Assignment

The students go on a Trivia Treasure Hunt in one or more of the categories--American History, Authors and Literature, Science and Nature, and Sports and Games.

Library Media Skills
- Learning to find specific information from reference materials
- Synthesizing information

Subject Curriculum Content
- Learning a skill needed for research in all curriculum areas

Resources and Materials
- Reference materials
- Question sheets for use with single category or index cards on which one question from each category has been typed
- Answer sheet

Activities
1. If more than one category will be used, the library teacher has one question from each category typed on index cards. Sheets of questions can be used if only one category will be covered. It will be helpful to have the cards or sheets laminated to be used by successive classes.
2. The library teacher leads a discussion of previous orientation sessions so that students can review the materials they have discovered and used. To preserve the Treasure Hunt aspect of this exercise, no reference materials are set aside.
3. The library teacher and the classroom teacher circulate to assist students and correct answers as they are completed.

Suggestion

This exercise may be done as a contest with a prize going to the student who finishes first or the student with the most correct answers at the end of the session.

ORIENTATION—LESSON #5

TRIVIA TREASURE HUNT—AMERICAN HISTORY

1. What was Harriet Tubman's name at birth?

2. In government, what is the New Deal?

3. What is the Sixth Amendment to the U.S. Constitution?

4. When did Arizona become a state?

5. In what year of the American Revolution did a fire destroy one-fourth of New York City?

6. What ship did Isaac Hull command in the War of 1812?

7. What was the name of the ship that hosted the Boston Tea Party?

8. Which state is known as the Equality State?

9. What college did President Chester Arthur attend?

10. Who were the two lawyers in the Scopes trial?

11. What was President John Adams' occupation after he left the presidency?

12. In what year did Congress make the "Pledge of Allegiance" part of its code for use of the flag?

13. What act created the Supreme Court?

14. Who was John Peter Zenger's lawyer at his trial for libel in 1735?

15. Members of what Indian tribe were massacred at Wounded Knee in 1890?

16. In what year did Congress enact a resolution naming the fourth Thursday of November as Thanksgiving?

17. How deep and long was the Erie Canal?

18. Who wrote the "Battle Hymn of the Republic"?

19. Who was Tory commander at the Battle of Brandywine Creek?

20. Who founded Boy Scouting in the United States?

21. How many electoral votes did John Kennedy and Richard Nixon get in the election of 1960?

22. Of what Indian tribe was Joseph Brant a chief?

23. What famous American song did Katherine Lee Bates write?

24. What was the first word said on the moon?

25. When was the first juvenile court established?

26. Who discovered Manhattan Island?

27. For what was Mrs. O'Leary's cow responsible?

28. What labor union was involved in the Homestead Strike of 1892?

29. In what year was the impeachment trial of President Andrew Johnson?

30. What was the fate of the Dalton brothers' gang?

31. From what law school did Clarence Darrow graduate?

32. What did John Eckert develop?

33. At what American university did Jonas Salk direct the work to develop the polio vaccine?

34. What was the government trying to stop when Sitting Bull was killed in 1890?

35. In what state was Andersonville, the Civil War prison?

ORIENTATION—LESSON #5

TRIVIA TREASURE HUNT—AMERICAN HISTORY—ANSWERS

1. Araminta Ross
2. relief, recovery, reform
3. speedy public trial in state where offense was committed
4. February 14, 1912
5. 1776
6. *Constitution*
7. the *Dartmouth*
8. Wyoming
9. Union College
10. Clarence Darrow and William Jennings Bryan
11. writer
12. 1942
13. the Judiciary Act of 1789
14. Andrew Hamilton
15. Sioux
16. 1941
17. 4 feet; 363 miles
18. Julia Ward Howe
19. Major Patrick Ferguson
20. William D. Boyce
21. 303 and 219
22. Mohawk
23. "America the Beautiful"
24. Houston
25. July 1, 1899
26. Giovanni da Verrazano
27. the great Chicago fire of October 8-9, 1871
28. the Amalgamated Association of Iron, Steel, and Tin Workers
29. 1868
30. 2 killed; 1 to prison becoming a law-abiding citizen after release
31. none; studied on his own
32. first advanced electronic computer
33. University of Pittsburgh
34. Ghost Dance ritual
35. Georgia

ORIENTATION—LESSON #5

TRIVIA TREASURE HUNT—AUTHORS AND LITERATURE

1. What book won the Pulitzer Prize for fiction in 1984?

2. What volume of Walt Whitman's poetry was published in nine separate editions?

3. How many Pulitzer Prizes did author William Faulkner win?

4. When did author Henry Thoreau move to Walden Pond?

5. What are the two cities in Dickens' *A Tale of Two Cities*?

6. Who is the Winged Horse in Greek mythology?

7. How many voyages does Sinbad the Sailor make?

8. What is unique about the Amazon warriors of Greek legend?

9. Who is Pecos Bill's true love?

10. Who is the housekeeper of Sherlock Holmes?

11. Who is the schoolteacher in Washington Irving's "The Legend of Sleepy Hollow"?

12. Shakespeare wrote in *Romeo and Juliet*, "Parting is such sweet . . ."

13. Name Louisa May Alcott's book in which Meg, Jo, Beth, and Amy are the main characters.

14. What play by Lorraine Hansberry won the New York Drama Critics Circle Award in 1959?

15. What was the name of the newspaper edited by Bret Harte?

16. What is the motto of the Three Musketeers?

17. Who is Oliver Twist's guide in thievery?

18. Who was Anne Frank hiding from?

19. What is the name of King Arthur's sword?

20. In what language was Chaucer's *Canterbury Tales* written?

21. Who was the King of England when Robin Hood lived in Sherwood Forest?

22. Who are Tom's owners in *Uncle Tom's Cabin*?

23. Who narrates the story in *The Adventures of Huckleberry Finn*?

24. In Longfellow's "Song of Hiawatha," to what tribe does Hiawatha belong?

25. When was the *New York Times* founded?

26. Who was the hero of *The Leatherstocking Tales* by James Fenimore Cooper?

27. What political symbols is Thomas Nast responsible for creating?

28. Who does Gulliver meet in Lilliput?

29. What two colleges did poet Robert Frost attend?

30. How many books make up Tolkein's *Fellowship of the Ring*?

31. How old was S. E. Hinton when she began *The Outsiders*?

32. What did the author E. L. Konigsburg train to be?

33. When and where was Robinson Crusoe born?

34. What is the name of Washington Irving's home in Tarrytown, New York?

35. Where did the author Herman Melville study?

TRIVIA TREASURE HUNT—AUTHORS AND LITERATURE—ANSWERS

1. *Ironweed*
2. *Leaves of Grass*
3. two: *A Fable* in 1955 and *The Reivers* in 1963
4. July 4, 1845
5. Paris and London
6. Pegasus
7. seven
8. The were all women.
9. Lightfoot Sue
10. Mrs. Hudson
11. Ichabod Crane
12. sorrow
13. *Little Women*
14. *A Raisin in the Sun*
15. *Overland Monthly*
16. "All for one and one for all"
17. Fagin
18. the Nazis
19. Excalibur
20. Middle English
21. Henry II
22. Shelby family
23. Huck
24. Ojibwas
25. 1851
26. Natty Bumppo
27. Democratic donkey and Republican elephant
28. little people
29. Dartmouth and Harvard
30. three
31. 15 or 16
32. chemist
33. 1632; York
34. Sunnyside
35. Albany Academy, Albany, New York

ORIENTATION—LESSON #5

TRIVIA TREASURE HUNT—SPORTS AND GAMES

1. What does a soccer player do when he or she tackles?

2. What Indian game was the basis for badminton?

3. How many times did the New York Yankees win the World Series between 1950 and 1960?

4. Where were the winter Olympic Games held in 1932 and in 1980?

5. When was the Heisman Trophy first awarded?

6. Who was the first track star to break the four-minute mile?

7. In chess, which piece can be moved only one square in any direction?

8. How high is a regulation basketball net?

9. What is the maximum number of clubs allowed in golf?

10. How many slots are in the home base of a Chinese checkers board?

11. What basketball team did Abe Saperstein found and coach?

12. Who played in the first American intercollegiate football game and when?

13. What is the oldest of football's bowl games?

14. What do the 4 H's stand for in the name 4-H Club?

15. What does the term *address* mean in golf?

16. Of what material is a golf ball made?

17. In rock climbing, what is the name of the technique in which a rope from the top of the climb holds the climber?

18. What are the three types of fencing?

19. How long are the sides of the square making up the official baseball diamond?

20. Who was the star of *Steamboat Willie*, Disney's first cartoon to use sound effects?

21. What kind of face did the clown Emmett Kelly have?

22. In what year did the Ringling Brothers and Barnum and Bailey circuses join to form one show?

23. Who invented the game of basketball, and when was it invented?

24. What is the weight of a regulation basketball?

25. Who is the "father of the bicycle"?

26. How many players does a rugby team have?

27. What is it called when a golfer moves the clubhead back and forth over the ball before a stroke?

28. How long does a minor penalty last in ice hockey?

29. How much does a hockey puck weigh?

30. What is the most powerful chess piece?

31. How many squares are there on a chessboard?

32. What is the height of a regulation tennis net?

33. In bowling, what is a turkey?

34. What is the snatch in weightlifting?

35. How far is it from base line to base line on a tennis court?

TRIVIA TREASURE HUNT—SPORTS AND GAMES—ANSWERS

1. takes ball away with the feet
2. poona
3. seven
4. Lake Placid, New York
5. 1935
6. Roger Bannister
7. King
8. 10 feet
9. 14
10. 10
11. Harlem Globetrotters
12. Princeton and Rutgers; November 6, 1869
13. Rose Bowl
14. head, heart, hands, health
15. Player is in position to hit ball.
16. rubber thread or band wrapped around core of water, silicone, nylon, or rubber
17. top-roping
18. foil, epee, and saber
19. 90 feet
20. Mickey Mouse
21. sad-faced hobo
22. 1919
23. Dr. James Naismith; 1891
24. 20-22 oz.
25. Baron Karl von Drais
26. 15
27. a waggle
28. 2 minutes
29. 5 1\2-6 oz.
30. Queen
31. 64
32. 3 feet
33. 3 strikes in a row
34. Lifter grips barbell with both hands and with one motion puts it over his head and locks his arms.
35. 78 feet

ORIENTATION—LESSON #5

TRIVIA TREASURE HUNT—SCIENCE AND NATURE

1. Why is the adrenal gland called the "gland of combat"?

2. How are dinosaurs classified in terms of their body structure?

3. What is the speed of light in a vacuum? (miles\second)

4. What is a mud puppy?

5. What are amberjacks?

6. How often do deer shed and renew their antlers?

7. What is a macaque? In what area of the world does it live?

8. What are the tusks of the elephant used as?

9. What is unique about the way the frog crab moves?

10. What is a langur?

11. What is the length of a marmoset's body in contrast to the length of its tail?

12. How many chambers are there in a nautilus shell?

13. How many bones are in your skeleton?

14. What is the natural home of a rabbit?

15. What eye problem do bulls have?

16. What instrument is used to measure earthquakes?

17. What have you get 10,000 of on your tongue?

18. What do you call a unit that measures loudness?

19. When a caterpillar attaches itself to a tiny twig and grows a hard skin, what is the hard skin called?

20. How far up is the ozone layer?

21. What part of the silkworm is used to obtain silk?

22. What are the three layers in the structure of the earth?

23. What are the three main classifications of fruit?

24. What is the smallest planet?

25. How many teeth do dogs have?

26. How large is the diameter of the earth around the equator?

27. How long do red blood cells live in the bloodstream?

28. Of what two metals is brass an alloy?

29. What are the castes, or classes of society, in an anthill?

30. What makes up 78 percent of our air?

31. What city does the Prime Meridian run through?

32. What is Mohs' scale?

33. What is the average depth, in feet, of the Pacific Ocean?

34. How much of the earth's surface is covered by water?

35. How many teeth does a human grow in a lifetime?

ORIENTATION—LESSON # 5

TRIVIA TREASURE HUNT—SCIENCE AND NATURE—ANSWERS

1. It goes into action in times of stress.
2. according to the structure of the hipbones
3. 186,282 miles\second
4. a type of salamander
5. fish
6. annually
7. a monkey; Asia
8. teeth
9. moves backwards
10. a monkey
11. 8 inch body; 12 inch tail
12. 30
13. 206
14. burrow
15. They're color blind.
16. seismograph
17. taste buds
18. decibel
19. a chrysalis
20. 30 km. or 20 miles
21. cocoon
22. crust, mantle, core
23. fleshy, stone (pits), dry
24. Mercury
25. 42
26. 7,926.7 miles
27. about 125 days
28. copper and zinc
29. queen, workers, males
30. nitrogen
31. Greenwich, England
32. a scale of ten common minerals in order of increasing hardness
33. 12,925
34. 70% or 3/4
35. 52 (20 baby teeth and 32 permanent)

Unit: Notetaking Techniques

Assignment

The student will critically read an article to extract important ideas and take notes in the prescribed manner.

Library Media Skills
- Notetaking using index cards
- Reading to extract important ideas
- Expressing ideas in an original manner

Subject Curriculum Content
- Learning a skill needed for research in all curriculum

Resources and Materials
- Explanation sheet
- Article from an encyclopedia, magazine, *School Issues Resource Series (SIRS)*, or *SIRS Digest*
- Sheet with blank note cards for practicing

Activities
1. The library teacher selects a brief article to be used for class practice. The article should be related to course material for the integrated subject.
2. The library teacher distributes explanation sheet and describes rationale and procedure for notetaking on cards. The class practices notetaking from the selected article.

NAME _____ PERIOD _____

DATE _____ **NOTETAKING TECHNIQUES**

NOTETAKING ON CARDS -- Some questions and answers

Why is it helpful to learn notetaking using index cards?

Using index cards helps you in the following ways:
1. You separate the important ideas from those that are not important, so you do not waste time taking notes on ideas you will not use.
2. You must be brief, so you spend less time writing than if you copied the information word for word.
3. Since the notes are in your own words you eliminate the danger of plagiarism.
4. It is easier to organize your notes. Separate ideas will be on separate cards making it a simple matter to shuffle cards into any order you wish.

What information should be included on each notecard?

1. Idea label -- description of information found on the card, helps with the card arranging
2. Source -- author, shortened title if no author is given
3. Page number
4. Note -- single idea or piece of information

What should the notecard look like?

Idea label	Source
	Page no.
Note	

How should the notes be taken?

1. Summary -- the most frequently used method of notetaking; the original idea in your own words
2. Short outline or list
3. Direct quotation --Used only when your own words would result in a misinterpretation or the quote will add meaning to your paper
    COPY THE ORIGINAL ACCURATELY -- REFERENCE IT

Are there any other hints that can be useful in notetaking?

1. Be brief; do not use complete sentences, just key words and phrases. Be sure to write enough so that you will understand your notes later.
2. Do not note obvious or commonly known ideas.
3. Sort the ideas as you are taking the notes; do not take notes on ideas you will not use.
4. Read at least a paragraph at a time before taking down a note. Reading smaller segments at a time usually results in too many notes.
5. Remember that the more carefully your notes are taken, the easier your paper will be to organize.

Unit: Bibliography

Assignment
The student will compile a bibliography on a selected topic. Library resources, including books, encyclopedias, magazines, videos, and computer software will be used.

Library Media Skills
- Identifying the correct components for specific bibliographic entries
- Compiling a bibliography using proper components, punctuation, and spacing

Subject Curriculum Content
- Learning a skill needed for research documentation in a particular subject area

Resources and Materials
- Classroom Connect's Citing Internet Resources: A how-to guide for referencing online sources in student bibliography
  http://www.classroom.net/classroom/CitingNetResources.html
- Bibliographic style sheet
- Worksheet
- Library sources

Activities
1. The library teacher presents the bibliographic style worksheet.
2. The students identify the components of each bibliographic entry on style sheet and fill in worksheet.
3. With assistance from the teachers, the students prepare bibliographic entries for each statement on the assignment sheet. Attention is paid to proper order, punctuation, and spacing.
4. For homework, students recopy entries in alphabetical order.

BIBLIOGRAPHIC STYLE SHEET

Book entries: One and two authors

Stanley, Jerry. <u>Children of the Dust Bowl: The True Story of the School of Weedpatch Camp</u>. New York: Crown Pub., Inc., 1992.

Moss, Joyce and Wilson, George. <u>Peoples of the World: North Americans</u>. Detroit: Gale Research, Inc., 1991.

Books in series entries: Book and electronic form

Honig, Donald. "Baseball." <u>World Book</u>. Vol. 2 (1998), 96-110.

"King Snake." <u>Marshall Cavendish International Wildlife Encyclopedia</u>. Vol. 12 (1990), 1367-1368.

"Jack London." <u>Grolier Electronic Encyclopedia</u>. Grolier Electronic Publishing, Inc., 1992. CD-ROM.

Magazine entries with and without author

Busch, Richard. "City at the Crossroads." <u>National Geographic Traveler</u>, 15 (March/April 1998): 98-113.

"Making Amends: Country Joe McDonald Honors the Veterans of a War He Scorned." <u>People Weekly</u>, 44 (November 27,1995): 146.

Videos

<u>Heaven and Earth</u>. Dir. Oliver Stone. United Artists, 1993.

"Women on the Kalahari." <u>In Search Of</u>. NBC, July 28, 1993.

Web Site

DiStefano, Vince. Guidelines for better writing. [On-line] Available http://www.usa.net/~vinced/home/better-writing.html, January 9, 1996.

Tips for organizing:
1. Alphabetize all entries by the first word , ignoring a, an, and the.
2. Write first word at margin of paper.
3. If entry takes more than one line, indent the second line and any that follow.
4. Do not use Style Sheet headings — book, encyclopedia, and so on, when compiling your bibliography.
5. If using a computer or word processor, titles may be italicized rather than underlined.

1. A bibliography entry for a book must include:

   1. _____

   2. _____

   3. _____

   4. _____

   5. _____

2. A bibliography entry for a book in series (book form) must include:

   1. _____

   2. _____

   3. _____

   4. _____

   5. _____

   6. _____

3. A bibliography entry for a book in series (electronic form) must include:

   1. _____

   2. _____

   3. _____

   4. _____

   5. _____

4. A bibliography entry for a periodical must include:

   1. _____

   2. _____

   3. _____

   4. _____

   5. _____

5. A bibliography entry for a video must include:

   1. _____

   2. _____

   3. _____

   4. _____

6. A bibliography entry for a web site must include:

   1. _____

   2. _____

   3. _____

   4. _____

Bibliography: Sources

Assignment Sheet: Sports

1. In 1994 Jeff Bennett and Scott Downey had a book called <u>The Complete Snowboarder</u> published by Ragged Mountain Press in Denver.

2. The <u>World Book Encyclopedia</u> article, "Baseball" written by Donald Honig for the 1998 edition appears in volume 2 on pages 124-139.

3. Lyons and Burford in New York published <u>The Cross-country Primer</u> by Laurie Gullion in 1990.

4. Johnette Howard wrote an article about women's hockey called "Golden Girls." Appearing in the March 2, 1998 issue of <u>Sports Illustrated</u> on pages 46-47, it can be found in volume 88.

5. <u>Let's Play Tennis with Tracy Austin, Cliff Drysdale, and Fred Stolle</u>. Dir. Dustin Andrew. Vue Productions, 1994 is a videocassette.

6. You found an article today called "My Dean Smith Story" at the web address of http://www.hoophall.com/hallfyi/hallguy.html. It was written by Brian Deutsch.

Unit: Searching the Internet

Assignment

After a brief presentation of some basic techniques used for searching the Internet, students will use these techniques with teacher direction. After completing teacher-directed exercise, students will search the Internet.

Library Media Skills

- Identifying tools to search the Internet for information
- Using two of these tools, Yahoo and Hot Bot, to search the Internet
- Using Boolean and proximity searching to locate information
- Comparing and contrasting the results

Subject Curriculum Content

- Learning a skill needed for research in all curriculum areas

Resources and Materials

- The Internet
- Worksheets

Activities

Day 1

1. Library teacher instructs the students in the basics of searching the Internet by using a web browser such as Netscape, Microsoft Internet Explorer, and so on, stressing the functions of the tool bar icons and the information on the home page.
2. Library teacher directs students through the use of Yahoo as the students complete the worksheet.
3. At completion the students discuss what they have learned and how they can apply this knowledge in researching subjects.

Day 2

4. Library teacher repeats the procedure for Hot Bot.
5. Discussion follows concerning the use of Hot Bot emphasizing its ability to broaden and narrow the topic. The advantages and disadvantages of the two search tools are compared and contrasted.
6. Students use both Yahoo and Hot Bot to research a topic of choice.

Suggestions

Because many students by the time they reach middle or junior high school are completely knowledgeable in searching the Internet, these students should buddy with the novices.

Though Yahoo and Hot Bot are referenced for this unit, the search engines of your choice can easily be substituted for them. The subject of the search can easily be changed as well.

NAME _____ PERIOD _____

DATE _____ **SEARCHING THE INTERNET**

Start your World Wide Web browser. Check the home page for the services provided.

    1. How many services or search engines were provided? _____

    2. Name three of these search engines.

        _____, _____, _____

Bring up Yahoo by typing www.yahoo.com in the location blank or by selecting it from the list provided.

Place the topic El Nino in the Yahoo location blank and search.

Answer:
    1. I found _____ categories and _____ sites.

    2. What categories for El Nino did you find?

        _____

        _____

        _____

    3. Click on the highlighted words in one of the web sites. Did you find information about

        your topic? _____

    4. Search in Yahoo's News Stories for El Nino. How many headlines did you find? _____

    5. Do a "people search" for Walt Disney. How many matches did you find? _____

Change to the search engine Hot Bot by typing www.hotbot.com or by selecting it from the list on your server's home page.

1. Search for "all the words" (AND). How many hits returned? _____

2. Search for "any of the words" (OR). How many hits returned? _____

3. Search for "the exact phrase." How many hits returned? _____

4. Search for "the title page." How many hits returned? _____

5. Do a Boolean search for El AND Nino AND NOT Science. How many hits returned?

   _____

6. Search for the exact phrase but only in Asia. How many hits returned? _____

7. Search for the exact phrase but only in North American sites. How many hits

   returned? _____

8. Search for the exact phrase but only in documents from the past week. How many hits

   returned? _____

9. Search for the person, Walt Disney. How many hits returned? _____

ART

Unit: A Historical Perspective on American Architecture

Integrated Subject: Art

Assignment

Students will learn about the various styles of American houses that have been popular through the history of American architecture. Then students will select architectural details that they admire and incorporate them into designs of their own.

Library Media Skills

- Finding information in print and nonprint resources
- Synthesizing information

Art Curriculum Content

- Understanding the historical development of the architecture of American houses
- Understanding the details that make each architectural style unique
- Understanding the influences on architectural styles through the years
- Incorporating details into original designs so that they are artistically and functionally effective

Resources and Materials

- *The American House--Styles of Architecture Coloring Book*
- *From Tepees to Towers*
- *All the Ways of Building*
- *Built in the U.S.A.*
- *Architecture of the Twentieth Century*
- *Open House in New England*
- *The Heritage of Early American Houses*
- *Houses in America*
- *Architectural Treasury of Early American Houses* (series)
- *White Pillars*
- *Colonial Houses*
- Architecture in America (photos)
  http://lcweb2loc.gov/detroit/archamer.html
- Slides showing various architectural styles
- Computer-aided design software, if available

Activities

1. The library teacher and the art teacher prepare slides that show various styles of American houses. A helpful book for this is Dover's *The American House— Styles of Architecture Coloring Book*. The following are the most popular styles for students to include in their designs:

49

-Saltbox House
-Cape Cod Cottage
-Log Cabin
-Georgian Transitional House (Students like the cupola!)
-German Stone House
-Greek Revival House
-Jefferson Classic House (as in Monticello)
-Carpenter's Gothic House
-Octagon House
-High Victorian Gothic House
-Queen Anne House
-Shingle House
-Prairie-style House (designed by Frank Lloyd Wright)
-Contemporary-style House

2. Prior to coming to the library, the art teacher has introduced architectural drawing by hand or with software, if available.

3. The art teacher and the library teacher show the slides to the class. During this presentation, students note styles and details that they particularly admire.

4. The library teacher introduces sources that the students will use to research architectural styles and details as the library teacher and the art teacher assist them.

5. Students complete their designs in art room or computer room.

Unit: The Influence of Classical Architecture on Local Buildings

Integrated Subject: Art

Assignment
      Students will locate definitions and draw simple sketches of architectural details that were first used in the architecture of Greece, Rome, and Egypt. Then they will view slides of local buildings identifying the architectural details they have researched.

Library Media Skills
- Finding information in print and electronic sources
- Synthesizing information

Art Curriculum Content
- Knowing about architectural features and details that originated in Greece, Rome, and Egypt
- Recognizing those features in local buildings
- Understanding the influences of classical architecture on local buildings

Resources and Materials
- *The Buildings of Ancient Egypt*
- *The Romance of Architecture*
- *From Tepees to Towers*
- *The First Book of Architecture*
- *All the Ways of Building*
- *Grand Constructions*
- *City*
- Architecture through the Ages
  http://library.advanced.org/10098/
- Greek Architecture
  http://communityhigh.org/katelevy/greek/greek.html
- Dictionaries
- Print and electronic encyclopedias
- Slides of local buildings
- List of architectural terms to be defined

Activities
1. The library teacher and the art teacher prepare slides of local buildings displaying features of classical origin.
2. The library teacher introduces sources that include definitions and illustrations of architectural terms. The terms to be researched may be listed on the chalkboard, or the list may be distributed to the students. At the discretion of the teachers, student

use of dictionaries and encyclopedias may be limited.

3. With the assistance of the library teacher and the classroom teacher, the students write the definitions and make simple sketches of the terms on their own paper. Students should be instructed to leave space between definitions so that names of local buildings can be inserted.

4. When students have completed the definitions and sketches, the library teacher and the classroom teacher review the definitions and show the slides of local buildings. Students identify the buildings and the classical features in their design. Students add the names of the buildings next to the appropriate definitions and sketches.

Suggestion

This unit may be done when students are studying the civilizations of Greece, Rome, and Egypt in social studies classes. In fact, in programs where students do not take art, it can be done as part of the social studies class itself.

Influence of Classical Architecture
Terms to Define

keystone

pilaster

molding or moulding

obelisk

pediment

Doric column

Ionic column

Corinthian column

ampitheater

arch

vault

dome

Unit: Art History, Art Appreciation

Integrated Subject: Art

Assignment

The students will use library resources and search strategies to locate information on an artist, his/her style, and his/her impact on the art world. The students will report findings in either a written report or another medium. The other medium may be a mobile, poster, picture book, video, or something else. Each report must be accompanied by a bibliography.

Library Media Skills

- Selecting appropriate resources for research
- Using research strategies, particular emphasis to be placed on the value of indexes and tables of contents
- Taking notes in a prescribed form
- Organizing information
- Writing a bibliography for all sources according to the prescribed form

Art Curriculum Content

- Learning the life of an artist and the style or styles the artist used
- Learning the artist's influence on the art world

Suggested Topics

Sandro Botticelli	Piet Mondrian
Georges Braque	Claude Monet
Alexander Calder	Grandma Moses
Mary Cassatt	Edvard Munch
Marc Chagall	Louise Nevelson
Salvador Dali	Georgia O'Keefe
Edgar Degas	Pablo Picasso
Leonardo da Vinci	Camille Pissarro
Francisco de Goya	Raphael
William De Kooning	Rembrandt
Eugene Delacroix	Frederick Remington
Albrecht Durer	Auguste Renoir
Maurits Escher	Diego Rivera
Paul Gauguin	Norman Rockwell
Winslow Homer	Auguste Rodin
Edward Hopper	Henri Rousseau
George Inness	Peter Paul Rubens
Jasper Johns	John Singer Sargent
Frida Kahlo	Georges Seurat
Wassily Kandinsky	Henri de Toulouse-Lautrec
Paul Klee	Vincent Van Gogh

Berthe Marisot
Henri Matisse
Michelangelo
Amedeo Modigliani

Jan Vermeer
Andy Warhol
Andrew Wyeth
Grant Wood

Resources and Materials

- *A New World History*
- *A History of Art*
- *American Art of Our Century*
- *Understanding Art*
- *The Story of Art*
- *Pop Art*
- *Your Art Heritage*
- *Impressionism*
- *History of Art*
- *Cubism*
- *Modern Painting*
- *Women Impressionists*
- *Masterpieces of American Painting*
- *Larousse Encyclopedia of Modern Art*
- *Current Biography*
- *Great Artists of the Western World* Series 1 & 2
- *Masterpieces of American Painting in the Metropolitan Museum of Art*
- WebMuseum network http://sunsite.unc.edu/louvre/
- Yahoo's list of artists http://www.yahoo.com/Arts/Art_History /Artists/

- *Art of Our Century*
- *Art*
- *A Child's History of Art*
- *American Art Now*
- *Fifty Centuries of Art*
- *17th & 18th Century Art*
- *Famous Paintings*
- *Twentieth Century Art*
- *Great Painters*
- *Surrealism*
- *American Painting*
- *The Story of Art for Young People*
- *Masters of Art*
- *Masterpieces of American Art*
- *McGraw-Hill Encyclopedia of World Biography*
- Individual biographies

Activities

1. The library teacher explains the use of sources, stressing the importance of indexes in art history books and the special uses of the reference sources.
2. The art and library teacher explain the kind of information to be collected.
3. The library teacher reviews notetaking and bibliography techniques.
4. The students take notes on cards.
5. The library teacher reviews the organization of the cards.
6. The art teacher checks the cards for completeness of information.
7. The students complete report and bibliography.

ENGLISH

Unit: Magazines

Integrated Subject: English

Assignment

Students evaluate magazines in different categories and complete worksheets.

Library Media Skills

- Reviewing various types of magazines
- Understanding that the mission of a magazine is reflected in its advertising, editorial policy, and content

English Curriculum Content

- Studying the styles of writing in advertising and articles in different types of magazines
- Drawing conclusions about ways in which this form of mass media appeals to readers

Resources and Materials

- Magazines from the library collection grouped according to the following types and placed at "stations":
    - news
    - youth
    - sports\health
    - travel\geography
    - general interest
    - technology\computer
    - home\craft
    - history
    - science\nature
    - consumer
- Worksheet

Activities

1. The library teacher initiates a discussion about periodicals that students read most often and the variety of magazines on the market.
2. The library teacher explains that the most successful magazines have a clear idea of their purpose and intended audience, which are kept in mind through ads, articles, and editorial policy.
3. The library teacher explains the worksheet, concentrating on how the students will characterize the audience to which the magazine appeals. For level of education or training, students can use the terms technical training, high school, two-year college, college, and advanced degree; for income level, the library teacher should provide

up-to-date breakdowns of lower, middle, and upper classes or use such general parameters as under $15,000, $15,000 - $75,000, and above $75,000.

4. The students should fill in the first sentence on the worksheet with the number of available stations and the number required.

5. The library teacher should divide the class so that everyone does not begin at the same station. Students can then move from one station to another of their choice as they complete the work.

NAME_____PERIOD_____

DATE_____**MAGAZINES**

_____stations have been set up, each with several magazines that are part of the same general category. You are to go to _____of the stations, select one magazine from each, and provide the following information about that magazine.

Station # _____Title of magazine_____

Title of one article_____

Four products advertised in the magazine_____

_____

Looking at the articles and products advertised, characterize the target audience for this magazine.

age_____ level of education or training_____

income level_____

special interests_____

_____

Station # _____ Title of magazine_____

Title of one article_____

Four products advertised in the magazine_____

_____

Looking at the articles and products advertised, characterize the target audience for this magazine.

age_____ level of education or training_____

income level_____

special interests_____

_____

****

Station # _____ Title of magazine_____

Title of one article_____

Four products advertised in the magazine_____

_____

Looking at the articles and products advertised, characterize the target audience for this magazine.

age_____ level of education or training_____

income level_____

special interests_____

_____

Unit: Poetic Devices

Assignment

After having learned about poetic devices in English class, students will browse the library's collection of poetry books to find examples of those devices and note them on the worksheet. Each student will then select a poem of at least eight lines that he\she especially likes. Students will read their poems to the class mentioning poetic devices used and their reasons for selecting the poems.

Library Media Skills

- Becoming aware of poetry collection
- Understanding the importance of citing sources, albeit informally

English Curriculum Content

- Understanding poetic devices and how to find them used in poems
- Practice in oral recitation of a poem

Resources and Materials

- An Index of Poem Titles
  http://library.utoronto.ca/www/utel/rp/indextitles.html
- Project Bartleby
  http://www.columbia.edu/acis/bartleby/index.html
- Poetry anthologies from the library's collection
- Worksheet

Activities

1. The library teacher introduces the lesson pointing out some notable books from the collection and explaining the worksheet. The library teacher might also read lines of poetry that include specific devices and ask students to identify them.
2. The library teacher points out the emotional nature of poetry and reads a favorite poem. Criteria for choosing a poem include subject matter of interest to the student, a strong emotional response, an understanding of the poem, and a confidence in being able to read it effectively.
3. The library teacher and the classroom teacher circulate to assist students.
4. The classroom teacher reviews principles of oral presentation.
5. Students complete worksheet and prepare presentations.

1. Locate the following poetic devices in the poetry anthologies in the library's collection. In the spaces provided, copy the line in which the device is used, write the title of the poem in quotation marks, and write the title of the anthology and underline it.

simile

quoted line_____

title of poem_____

title of anthology_____

metaphor

quoted line_____

title of poem_____

title of anthology_____

personification

quoted line_____

title of poem_____

title of anthology_____

alliteration

quoted line_____

title of poem_____

title of anthology_____

onomatopoeia

quoted line_____

title of poem_____

title of anthology_____

2. Find a poem of at least eight lines that appeals to you and that you think you could do a good job of reading aloud. The poem's subject might be of interest to you, or the poem could make you feel a certain way. In your oral presentation, you will be reading the poem, noting poetic devices, and discussing your reasons for choosing the poem. Either copy the poem, or have it photocopied.

title of poem_____

title of anthology_____

page number_____

Unit: Mythology

Integrated Subject: English

Assignment

After using library resources to research myths and their relationships to the skies, the student will prepare a research paper and a classroom oral report.

Library Media Skills

- Checking indexes and table of contents to identify appropriate sources
- Using illustrations, charts and maps to locate and sketch major constellations
- Extracting and reporting relevant information
- Compiling a bibliography in correct form

Social Studies Curriculum Content

- Demonstrating a knowledge of the names and locations of the major constellations which relate to the Greek myths
- Engaging in library research regarding the constellation of their choice
- Preparing projects using the results of their research and presenting them to other groups of students using selected media (film, slides, video, written papers, plays, etc.)

Suggested Topics

- See student assignment sheet

Resources and Materials

- *Mythology: An Illustrated Encyclopedia*
- *A Guide to the Gods*
- *Illustrated Encyclopedia of Mythology*
- *New Larousse Encyclopedia Of Mythology*
- *A Companion to World Mythology*
- *Standard Dictionary of Folklore Mythology and Legend*
- *Redshift2*
- Encyclopedia Mythica
  http://www.pantheon.org/mythica/
- The Night Sky/Topical Index of Gods and Goddesses
  http://www.windows.umich.edu/the_universe/constellations.html
- The Constellations and their Stars
  http://www.astro.wisc.edu/~dolan/constellations/
- Mythology books
- Astronomy books
- Encyclopedias
- Handout and test

Activities

1. After completing work in Greek mythology, the subject teacher will introduce the research project.
2. The librarian will introduce the students to the night sky through a planetarium visit, a video, or an oral presentation.
3. The library teacher will familiarize students with materials. The students will research myths and their relationship to the skies.
4. The students will prepare and present their reports.

NAME _____ PERIOD _____

DATE _____ **MYTHOLOGY: ASSIGNMENT SHEET**

Your turn to "discover" the ancient skies

As a concluding mythology activity, you will be researching and reporting on constellations. You will be discovering the stories behind these groups of stars, learning the arrangement of these stars in our sky, and reporting this information to the class.

Requirements for the Research Paper
1. Five pages (minimum)
   a. Cover page
   b. Two-page mythological story, including how it ended up in the sky
   c. Sketch or drawing of the constellation
   d. Star chart of the constellation
   e. Bibliography (two sources)
2. Oral report to the class

Possible Topics
- Pleiades
- Sagittarius (scorpion)
- Cephius/Cassiopeia
- Perseus
- Aquila
- Pegasus
- Scorpius
- Orion
- Cepheus
- Ariadne (the crown)
- The Wagoner
- Virgo
- Procyon (the little dog)
- Pisces
- Auriga
- Other (with prior approval)

Possible Sources and Locations
- Mythology books
- Astronomy books
- Reference books
- Encyclopedias

NAME _____ PERIOD _____

DATE _____ **MYTHOLOGY: EVALUATION SHEET**

MYTHOLOGY RESEARCH REPORT

Requirements	Possible Points	Student Points	Teacher Points
Cover Page	5	_____	_____
Mythological Story	35	_____	_____
Sketch of Constellation	10	_____	_____
Star Chart	10	_____	_____
Bibliography	20	_____	_____
Oral Report	20	_____	_____

Comments:

Choose the letter of the answer that best completes each statement. Fill in the matching space on the answer sheet.

1. In the Greek language, the word "zodiac" means
   a. star group.
   b. animal circle.
   c. knowledge of the future.

2. The scientific term for the sun's apparent yearly path is
   a. the ecliptic.
   b. the equator
   c. the meridian.

3. According to the ancient Greeks, the god who drives the chariot around the sun daily is
   a. Poseidon.
   b. Zeus.
   c. Apollo.

4. The twins who make up the constellation Gemini are
   a. Castor and Pollux.
   b. Athene and Arachne.
   c. Orpheus and Eurydice.

5. Europa was "taken for a ride" by Zeus in the form of
   a. a swan.
   b. a dolphin.
   c. a bull.

6. Ursa Major is another name for the constellation
   a. Leo the lion.
   b. Big Dipper.
   c. Libra the scales.

7. The mother bear forever points toward Polaris, an important star better known as
   a. the north star.
   b. the little star.
   c. the southern cross.

8. The dolphin was immortalized as a constellation because
   a. it was an important food source to the ancient Greeks.
   b. it was a graceful and beautiful animal.
   c. it saved the life of Arion a famous musician.

9. The story of Orpheus and Eurydice is commemorated in the stars by the constellation
   a. Ursa Major.
   b. Delphinius.
   c. Lyre.

10. According to the Greek myths, Cygnus the swan was placed in the sky because
    a. the diving of Phaethon's friend reminded Zeus of a swan.
    b. the favorite bird of Zeus was the swan.
    c. a swan once saved the life of Zeus.

11. The shape V is a conventional way of representing
    a. the head of a bull.
    b. a swan's wing.
    c. a dolphin's tail.

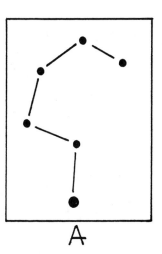

A

Identify the constellation illustrated in each of the sketches:

1. Sketch A is part of the constellation
   a. Ursa Major.
   b. Leo the lion.
   c. Gemini the twins.

2. Sketch B is the constellation
   a. Gemini the twins.
   b. Taurus the bull.
   c. Leo the lion.

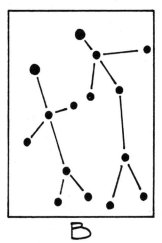

B

3. Sketch C is the constellation
   a. Leo the lion.
   b. Taurus the bull.
   c. Ursa Major.

4. Sketch D is part of the constellation
   a. Taurus the bull.
   b. Gemini the twins.
   c. Ursa Major.

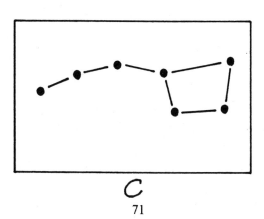

C

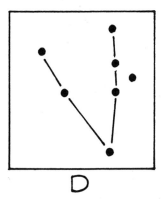

D

Unit: Folklore

Integrated Subject: English

Assignment

     Students choose from among twelve options for the study of folklore defined in its broad sense as many forms of spoken and written tradition including ceremonies, music, weather lore, proverbs, food lore, and others. Students research their topics and organize their information into a booklet.

Library Media Skills
- Locating information in print and non-print sources
- Synthesizing and organizing information

English Curriculum Content
- Greater understanding of traditional culture and its varied forms

Resources and Materials
- Books on the history of food, weather lore, plants, tongue twisters, natural medicine, holidays, art, folk music, toys, and hex signs. The volumes of *Foxfire* are especially valuable.
- Magazines, especially *Early American Life*
- CD's, cassettes, and records of folk music
- Handout explaining the options for the project

Activities
1. In the classroom, students have been reading, discussing, and writing tall tales, legends, and fables.
2. On their first day in the library, the library teacher introduces the project to the class, explaining the options and the sources that could be used for the study of each one. Each student receives a handout.
3. Sufficient time should be allowed for students to collect information on the topics they select. Research time may take up to one week in the library with the library teacher and classroom teacher assisting students.

Folklore: Handout

Choices for Folklore Project

The study of folklore includes the study of many forms of spoken and written tradition, including feasts, ceremonies, dances, art, crafts, games, superstitions, weather lore, medicine, food lore and proverbs.
- Select one of the following topics.
- Gather information on that topic.
- Organize your information.
- Present your information in the form of a booklet that is informative as well as attractive.

1. Many of our popular dishes were created in unusual ways and have names that are historically significant. Find out about several of these (such as, Boston cream pie, hush puppies, baked Alaska).

2. Although we are accustomed to sophisticated methods of weather forecasting, early people had their own natural ways to predict the weather. Find out about several of these.

3. More and more, we are coming to appreciate what ordinary plants can give to us. Look up plants that are commonly grown in this region, find out what uses they have beyond their beauty. Include explanations for their names and their uses.

4. Tongue twisters have been passed down by word of mouth for generations. Make a collection of tongue twisters. If possible, make a tape of those you can say.

5. Long before high-tech medical care was available, people used natural and simple ways to get rid of ailments. Make a booklet explaining several of these.

6. Many of our holidays and\or customs began in unique and interesting ways. Find out about the origin of several of our holidays (such as April Fools' Day) and customs (such as mistletoe).

7. Every group in our society or history has folk songs that began in interesting or unusual ways. Include folk songs with interesting origins.

Include photocopies of the sheet music in your booklet. If possible, make a tape of some of the folk songs covered in your booklet.

8. Make a booklet in which you reproduce and describe the meaning of several hex signs from the Pennsylvania Dutch. Include also a design of your own, making sure it is original; explain what it means to you.

9. Read a tall tale about a bigger-than-life character, and discuss that person's amazing feats.   Then create your own tall tale with your own original hero or heroine.

10. Fables are usually told by animals who speak as humans and usually teach a lesson or present a moral. Read and discuss one of *Aesop's Fables*. Then write your own fable using a moral of your choice or one of those listed below:
   •Better late than never.
   •The early bird catches the worm.
   •Don't put off until tomorrow what you can do today.
   •Haste makes waste.
   •It is better to give than to receive.
   •Experience is the best teacher.

11. Legends are often based on real people, but, as they grow, they may not be historically accurate. Read a legend and discuss it. Then write your own legend about a real person who interests you (an athlete, humanitarian, and so on).

12. Fairy tales were originally passed down by word of mouth and are stories of magic and enchantment. Read some and write your own.

Unit: Favorite Authors

Integrated Subject: English

Assignment

Each student will select a favorite author and research the author's life and the effect of the author's life experiences upon his\her work. This information will be written as a formal research essay with parenthetical references used as necessary and a bibliography. Each student will read an additional book by the author and also give an oral presentation from the point of view of a character from one of the author's books.

Library Media Skills

- Finding information in print and electronic sources
- Synthesizing and taking notes on notecards
- Organizing information
- Using parenthetical references as necessary
- Preparing a bibliography

English Curriculum Content

- Information on the lives of authors and the influences of their experiences on their work
- Techniques for writing a formal essay
- Techniques for making an oral presentation

Suggested Topics

- Any contemporary, modern, or classic author

Resources and Materials

- *Junior Discovering Authors* (on compact disc)
- *Something about the Author*
- *Junior Authors and Illustrators*
- *Authors and Artists for Young Adults*
- *Major Authors and Illustrators for Children and Young Adults*
- *Speaking for Ourselves, I* and *II*
- *Writers for Children*
- *Twentieth Century Authors*
- *American Authors 1600-1900*
- *Twentieth Century Children's Writers*
- *British Authors*
- *McGraw-Hill Encyclopedia of World Biography*
- *Current Biography*
- *American Biographies*

- *Literary History of the United States*
- *Oxford Companion to English Literature*
- *Oxford Companion to American Literature*
- *Writers' America*
- *Readers' Guide*, *Proquest* (or other periodical index to locate articles)
- Yahoo's Author list: Fiction
  http://www.yahoo.com/Arts/Humanities/Literature/Genres/Literary_Fiction/Auth
- Yahoo's Author list: Children's
  http://www.yahoo.com/Arts/Humanities/Literature/Genres/Children_s/Authors/
- Children's Literature Web Guide: Authors on the Web
  http://www.acs.ucalgary.ca/~dkbrown/authors.html
- Handout with ideas for research
- Books by chosen authors

Activities

1. The library teacher introduces the topic and discusses handout, which gives suggestions for research.
2. The library teacher reviews reference materials discussing specialized indexing for specific materials.
3. Each student selects an author to research. This author should be one whose work the student enjoys. The student should select another of the author's books to read as a homework assignment during the research time.
4. The library teacher reviews notetaking and bibliography.
5. The library teacher and the classroom teacher assist students in locating and synthesizing information.
6. After a few days of research, the library teacher introduces parenthetical references. The library teacher and the classroom teacher check notecards.
7. The library teacher reviews organization of notecards and the writing of an\ outline, list, or webbing\branching chart as methods of organization.
8. The students write their rough drafts, which are checked by the library teacher and the classroom teacher.
9. The classroom teacher reviews techniques for oral presentation.
10. The students complete their final drafts and prepare their oral presentations.

Favorite Authors: Handout

Some Ideas for Researching Favorite Authors

1. Where and when was the author born?

2. Describe the author's family.

3. Describe any significant experiences the author had as a child. Was the author's childhood unique in any way?

4. Describe the author's education.

5. When did the author start writing?

6. Describe the author as an adult, including personality, looks, interests, family life, and so on.

7. Explain the important influences on your author's life. Are these reflected in the author's writing?

8. Discuss the disappointments that your author experienced. Are these reflected in the author's writing?

9. Discuss the triumphs that were significant to your author. Are these reflected in the author's writing?

10. When did your author receive recognition for his/her writing? Did this recognition come in the author's lifetime?

11. What did your author say about his/her writing?

12. Is your author known to have used specific themes in his/her writing?

13. What kind of characters did your author create?

14. How did your author reflect the times in which he/she lived? Did any major events of the time appear directly in the writing?

15. When, where, and how did your author die?

Unit: African Americans in Arts and Letters

Integrated Subject: English

Assignment

Students will research an African-American artist of their own choice and prepare an oral presentation that includes a biography and an example of the artist's work appropriate to the art form involved.

Library Media Skills
- Finding information in print and electronic sources
- Synthesizing and organizing information

English Curriculum Content
- Understanding of the role African-American artists have played in the development of various art forms
- Techniques of making an oral presentation

Suggested Topics
- See accompanying handout.

Resources and Materials
- *Current Biography* (on compact disc or in book form)
- *McGraw-Hill Encyclopedia of World Biography*
- *Voices of Triumph* , especially volume entitled *Creative Fire*
- *Harlem Renaissance*
- NBC's Club Noir
  http://www.nbc.com/clubnoir/
- Periodicals
- Biographies and collective biographies
- Electronic encyclopedias
- Compact discs, records, and tapes of music
- Books on jazz, literature, and art
- List of individuals suggested for research

Activities
1. The library teacher introduces project. Some examples of the work of artists should be shown and listened to. Students may need some time to explore various artists and should be given free choice to select artists that interest them.
2. The library teacher passes out the listing of suggested artists.
3. The library teacher explains the use of special resources emphasizing unique indexing systems and use of equipment and electronic resources.
4. The students collect information about the lives and artistic endeavors of their chosen

artists while the library teacher and the classroom teacher assist them in finding and synthesizing appropriate information.

5. The classroom teacher reviews organization of material and principles of oral presentation.

6. Students make presentations to their classes.

Suggestion

If scheduling permits, this unit can be done in English class while the Civil Rights Movement is being done in social studies class.

African Americans in Arts and Letters:
Topics for Presentation

Anderson, Marian—singer

Angelou, Maya—poet

Armstrong, Louis—musician

Basie, Count—musician

Bontemps, Arna—author

Brooks, Gwendolyn—author

Cullen, Countee—poet

Dunbar, Paul Laurence—poet, novelist

Ellington, Duke—musician

Ellison, Ralph—author

Fitzgerald, Ella—singer

Franklin, Aretha—singer

Gillespe, Dizzy—musician

Giovanni, Nikki—poet

Hansberry, Lorraine—playright

Holiday, Billie—singer

Horne, Lena—singer

Hughes, Langston—poet, author

Hurston, Zora Neale—author

Jackson, Mahalia—singer

Joplin, Scott—composer

Lee, Spike—director

McDaniel, Hattie—actress

Morrison, Toni—author

Poitier, Sidney—actor

Rainey, Ma—singer

Ringgold, Faith—artist

Robeson, Paul—actor

Smith, Bessie—singer

Walker, Alice—author

Wilson, August—playright

Wright, Richard—author

Unit: Novels — Literary Criticism

Integrated Subject: English

Assignment

After selecting and reading a book by a chosen author, the student will prepare a critical review of the book. The review will include pertinent facts about the author.

Library Media Skills
- Selecting and using biographical reference sources
- Using cross references
- Finding specific sources of information
- Practicing and using techniques of notetaking
- Selecting and reading a book by the student's chosen author

English Curriculum Content
- Practicing listening skills
- Reviewing and practicing techniques for organizing information
- Recognizing the relationship between an author's life and his/her works
- Writing a book review

Resources and Materials
- *Who's Who in America*
- *Current Biography*
- *Twentieth Century Authors*
- *American Authors 1600-1900*
- *Something About the Author*
- *Authors of Books for Young People*
- *Junior Author Series*
- *Speaking for Ourselves*
- *Junior Discovering Authors*
- *School Library Journal, Horn Book, Booklist, English Journal*, and other professional journals
- Bookwire Reviews
  http://www.bookwire.com/reviews/
- The Hungry Mind Review
  http://www.bookwire.com/hmr/
- The New York Times Book Review
  http://www.nytimes.com/books/
- Carol Hurst's Children's Literature Site
  http://www.carolhurst.com/
- Kiddie Lit on the Net
  http://www://kn.pacbell.com/wired/KidLit/Kid.ht.

- Washington Post Book World
  http://www.washingtonpost.com/wp-srv/WPlate/m-bookworld.html
- Handout — Author list

Activities

1. The subject teacher introduces the research unit.
2. The subject teacher acquaints students with sources containing critical book reviews.
3. The students read and discuss a number of book reviews to learn the important elements of a good review.
4. The library teacher introduces appropriate biographical tools.
5. The students practice listening and notetaking skills during the introductory lectures.
6. The students select and read a book by the chosen author.
7. Using appropriate sources, the students research biographical information about the chosen author and complete a critical book review.

Novels: Handout
Authors to Write About

TEEN LIVING
Judie Angell
Alice Block
Francesca Lia Block
Judy Blume
Nancy Bond
Frank Bonham
Robin Brancato
Sue Ellen Bridgers
Betsy Byars
Beverly Cleary
Vera Cleaver
Hila Colman
Barbara Conklin
Ellen Conford
Paula Danziger
Barbara Girion
Lynn Hall
Nat Hentoff
S. E. Hinton
Isabelle Holland
Hadley Irwin
M. E. Kerr
John Knowles
Madeleine L'Engle
Lois Lowry
Harry Mazer
Norma Mazer
Gloria Miklowitz
John Neufield
Zibby Oneal
Francine Pascal
Katherine Patterson
Richard Peck
Marjorie Rawlings
Willo Roberts
Cynthia Rylant
Marilyn Sachs
Zilpha Snyder
Jerry Spinelli
Todd Strasser
Mildred Taylor
John Rowe Townsend
Cynthia Voigt
Rosemary Wells
Paul Zindel

MYSTERY
C. S. Adler
Joan Aiken
John Bellairs
Jay Bennett
Ernest Bethancourt
Agatha Christie
Lois Duncan
Virginia Hamilton
Stephen King
Joan Nixon
Christopher Pike
Edgar Allen Poe
Ellen Raskin
R. L. Stine
Patricia Windsor

SCIENCE FICTION
Isaac Asimov
Ray Bradbury
John Christopher
Arthur Clarke
Robert Heinlein
H. M. Hoover
Andre Norton
Allen Nourse
George Orwell
William Sleator
John Rowe Townsend
Jules Verne

FANTASY
Doug Adams
Lloyd Alexander
Terry Brooks
Susan Cooper
David Eddings
Paul Fleischman
Mollie Hunter
Ursula LeGuin
Anne McCaffrey
Robin McKinley
Mildred Ann Pierce
Mary Stewart
J. R. R. Tolkien
Jane Yolen

OTHER
Robert Cormier
Harper Lee
John Steinbeck
James Herriot

HISTORICAL FICTION
Avi
Natalie Babbit
Patricia Beatty
Christopher Collier
James L. Collier
Howard Fast
James Forman
Bette Greene
Irene Hunt
Scott O'Dell
Conrad Richter
Elizabeth Speare
Rosemary Sutcliffe
Theodore Taylor
Yoshiko Uchida
Jill Patom Walsh
Robert Westall
Leonard Wibblerly

ADVENTURE
Fred Gipson
William Golding
James Houston
Jim Kjelgaard
Louis L'Amour
Jack London
Harry Mazer
Farley Mowat
Gary Paulsen
Robert Louis Stevenson
Mark Twain
Robb White

SPORTS
Bruce Brooks
Robert Lipsyte
Walter Myers

HUMOR
Ellen Conford
Helen Cresswell
Paula Danziger
Gordon Korman
Richard Peck
Kin Platt
Mary Rodgers

FOREIGN LANGUAGE

Unit: Travel Tips

Integrated Subject: Foreign Language

Assignment

Using appropriate references, the students investigate information about a specific country in order to design a travel brochure.

Library Media Skills
- Locating and using reference sources
- Synthesizing information and taking notes on cards
- Preparing a bibliography

Foreign Language Curriculum Content
- Extracting practical information needed to go to a country that uses the language being studied
- Reporting the data in a travel brochure

Suggested Topics

Countries

French-speaking	German-speaking	Spanish-speaking	
France	Germany	Argentina	Mexico
Belgium	Austria	Bolivia	Nicaragua
Switzerland	Switzerland	Chile	Panama
Luxembourg	Luxembourg	Colombia	Paraguay
Canada	Liechtenstein	Costa Rica	Peru
Martinique		Cuba	Puerto Rico
Guadeloupe		Ecuador	Dominican Republic
Haiti		El Salvador	Uruguay
Tahiti		Spain	Venezuela
Senegal		Philippines	
Ivory Coast		Guatemala	
Monaco		Honduras	

Resources and Materials
- *Background Notes*
- *Culturgrams*
- *World and its People*
- Yahoo's Countries list
  http://www.yahoo.com/Regional/Countries/
- U.S. Department of State Background Notes
  http://www.state.gov/www/background_notes/index.html
- Library of Congress country studies
- http://lcweb2.loc.gov/frd/cs/cshome.html

- Microsoft Expedia
  http://expedia.msn.com/daily/home/default.hts
- Africa Guide
  http://www.sas.upenn.edu/Africa_Studies/Home-Page/AFR_GIDE.html
- Latin American Studies
- http://lanic.utexas.edu/las.html
- Travel periodicals
- Almanacs
- Pamphlet files (including materials from embassies)
- Travel guides
- Encyclopedia

Activities
1. The subject teacher assists students in selecting countries.
2. The library teacher introduces the assignment, distributing assignment booklet.
3. The students discuss information they should know about a country before traveling.
4. The library teacher explains materials that could be used, reviews notetaking and bibliography skills.
5. In the library, the students locate appropriate sources, scan for information, and take notes.
6. The booklet is completed from notes as a homework assignment.

YOU ARE GOING ON

A TRIP TO

_____

ASSIGNMENT:

Prepare a booklet of travel tips for yourself.

Date due: _____

REQUIREMENTS:

1. Use at least two sources for your information.

2. If you use a general encyclopedia, you will in-clude it as your third reference.

3. Collect your information on note cards.

4. Include a bibliography of the sources you used.

WHAT KIND OF INFORMATION SHOULD YOU GET BEFORE YOU LEAVE ON YOUR TRIP?

Kind of money /exchange rate

Climate/what clothing to bring

Manners/greetings

Health/shots you need

TO FIND THIS INFORMATION, LOOK IN SEVERAL SOURCES INCLUDING THE FOLLOWING:

The World and Its People

Background Notes

Culturgrams

Travel magazines

Almanacs

Pamphlet file

Books and travel guides

Encyclopedias

On-line services

Unit: Current Events in Foreign Countries

Integrated Subject: Foreign Language

Assignment

After selecting a country in which the foreign language being studied is spoken, the students locate an article relating to life in that country and complete a worksheet.

Library Media Skills
- Reviewing the use of cross references and key word terms
- Using magazine indexes in book or electronic form
- Completing a correct bibliography entry for the form used
- Skimming an article to locate main and supporting ideas

Foreign Language Curriculum Content
- Learning of current events in a country speaking the language being studied
- Broadening student's knowledge of the culture of that specific country

Resources and Materials
- Yahoo International Headlines
  http://www.yahoo.com/headlines/international/
- Magazine indexes, print or electronic
- Magazine articles
- Worksheet

Activities
1. The language teacher suggests countries for student investigation during introduction
2. The library teacher reviews the use of magazine indexes, stressing the use of key word searches and cross references.
3. Students locate an article in a magazine subscribed to by the library, skim the article, and the complete the worksheet.

NAME _____ PERIOD _____

DATE _____ **CURRENT EVENTS IN FOREIGN COUNTRIES**

Using magazine indexes, locate an article on your country appearing in a magazine. The issue date of the magazine must be within the last five years.

Write the bibliographic information for the article in the proper form.

_____

_____

_____

What is the main idea of the article?

_____

_____

_____

List ten supporting ideas that develop the article.

_____

_____

_____

_____

_____

_____

_____

_____

_____

_____

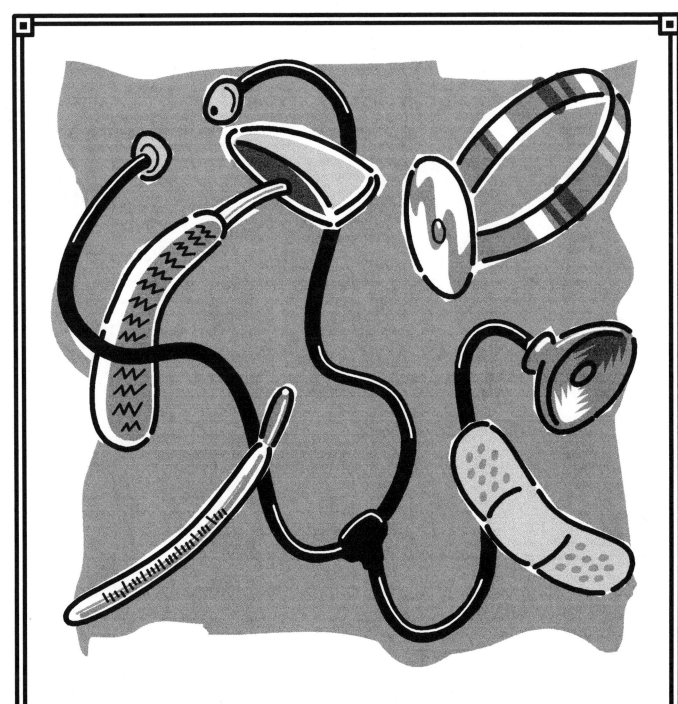

HEALTH

Unit: Disease Research

Integrated Subject: Health

Assignment

After researching a topic on disease or mental health, the student will complete an oral or written report covering causes, symptoms, treatments, and those people most commonly afflicted. A correct bibliography will be included.

Library Media Skills

- Identifying and selecting sources relating to the topic
- Extracting relevant information
- Synthesizing information
- Taking and organizing notes using prescribed procedures
- Compiling a correct bibliography

Health Curriculum Content

- Locating library resources pertinent to the study of the health curriculum
- Acquiring knowledge about a specific health topic

Suggested Topics

AIDS	Allergies
Alzheimer's disease	Anorexia nervosa
Arthritis	Asthma
Autism	Bronchitis
Cancer (lung, colon, skin, etc.)	Cerebral palsy
Cirrhosis	Coronary thrombosis
Cystic fibrosis	Dyslexia
Eczema	Encephalitis
Epilepsy	Glaucoma
Heart disease	Hodgkin's disease
Kleptomania	Leprosy
Leukemia	Meningitis
Multiple sclerosis	Muscular dystrophy
Obesity	Osteoporosis
Paranoia	Phlebitis
Rheumatoid arthritis	Scoliosis
Sickle-cell anemia	Syphilis
Viruses	

Resources and Materials

- *The Complete Home Medical Encyclopedia*
- *The Encyclopedia of Health and the Human Body*
- *Family Health and Medical Guide*
- *The Incredible Machine*
- *The Body in Question*

- *The Rand McNally Atlas of the Body and Mind*
- *The Marshall Cavendish Illustrated Encyclopedia of Family Health*
- *Family Doctor* (CD-ROM)
- Diseases, Disorders and Related Topics
  http://www.mic.ki.se/Diseases/index.html
- MedicineNet
  http://www.medicinenet.com/
- Yahoo's list of Diseases and Conditions
  http://www.yahoo.com/Health/Diseases_and_Conditions/
- Centers for Disease Control
  http://www.cdc.gov/diseases/diseases.html
- Mayo Clinic Health Oasis
  http://www.mayohealth.org
- General encyclopedias
- Health-related periodicals

Activities

1. The students receive an explanation of the assignment by the classroom teacher.
2. The students select an appropriate topic.
3. The library teacher briefly introduces the library sources for the topic.
4. The students complete research taking notes on the information.
5. The students report in a manner approved by the classroom teacher.

Unit: Substance Abuse

Integrated Subject: Health

Assignment

Working in groups of four, students prepare a research strategy, complete the research, and design an intervention program. Each student completes an individual bibliography.

Library Media Skills
- Using magazine and *SIRS* indexes
- Reading articles and synthesizing information
- Compiling a bibliography

Health Curriculum Content
- Obtaining information concerning drug abuse among the young and about intervention programs
- Using information to design an intervention program

Resources and Materials
- *Social Issues Resources Series* in book and electronic form
- Partnership for a Drug-Free America
  http://www.drugfreeamerica.org/
- Web of Addictions
  http://www.well.com/user/woa/
- Addiction Research Foundation
  http://www.arf.org/isd/info.html
- Magazine indexes in book and electronic forms

Activities
- The classroom teacher introduces the assignment to the students.
- The library teacher teaches or reviews the usage of magazine and *SIRS* indexes.
- The students locate and read articles containing information concerning topic.
- In groups of four, the students design an intervention program.
- The students select a spokesperson who presents program to the class.
- Individual bibliographies are handed in.

HOME
ECONOMICS

Unit: *Consumer Reports*

Integrated Subject: Home Economics

Assignment

Students will select a product or service that has been covered in an issue of the *Consumer Reports* magazine. Then they will use a periodical index to locate the appropriate issue of the magazine and complete a worksheet.

Library Media Skills

- Using a periodical index
- Learning about the range of products covered and the thoroughness and impartiality of *Consumer Reports*

Home Economics Curriculum Content

- Learning that consumers should research items before purchase
- Learning that one source for consumer information is *Consumer Reports*

Resources and Materials

- Issues of *Consumer Reports* magazine
- Periodical index (in book or compact disc form)
- Worksheet

Activities

1. The library teacher prepares a list of products and services that have been covered in the magazine. This will eliminate the frustration of students choosing products or services that the magazine has not covered.
2. The library teacher introduces the lesson stressing the wide range of items covered, the thoroughness of the research, and the impartiality of the presentation.
3. The library teacher reviews the strategies for using a periodical index and points out that the students will be following the same process for this lesson that they will follow later on when they need information on a product or service.
4. Students, working in pairs, select a product or service that they wish to research.
5. Student teams look up the products in the magazine index and request the issue of the magazine that they need.
6. Students complete the worksheet. At the discretion of the classroom teacher and the library teacher, the worksheet may be done either by each student or by the team.

NAME_____PERIOD_____

DATE_____*CONSUMER REPORTS*

Researching a Product or Service Using a Periodical Index and *Consumer Reports*

Product or service_____

Periodical index_____

Date of *Consumer Reports* issue_____Pages of article_____

1. Name three brand names that were tested.

2. Name three qualities or features of the product or service that was examined or tested.

3. Is there a rating chart?_____ If there is a rating chart, explain how it is arranged.

4. What brand names were recommended?

5. *Consumer Reports* looks at many different kinds of products and services. Look at the articles in your issue of the magazine. Name the products and services tested and reviewed according to the following categories noting that not all of the categories will be covered in each issue:

food_____

household products (detergents, etc.)_____

personal care products_____

appliances_____

entertainment_____

tools\outdoor products_____

health\fitness_____

auto_____

services (travel, shopping, etc.)_____

other_____

Unit: Career Exploration

Integrated Subject: Home Economics

Assignment

Using the biographical tool *Current Biography*, the students investigate the life of a person who is practicing a career that interests them. The students complete a brief worksheet showing the information gained.

Library Media Skills

- Using the "Index by Profession" in *Current Biography*
- Becoming familiar with the layout of the yearbook and the types of information presented in the articles

Home Economics Curriculum Content

- Exploring a career by reading about a person actually practicing that career
- Learning the many routes a person can take to reach a career goal
- Learning that many successful people have changed career directions and that this is acceptable and often desirable

Resources and Materials

- *Current Biography*
- Worksheet

Activities

1. The library teacher explains the principles and uses of *Current Biography*, focusing on the "Index by Profession" chart.
2. The students select a person involved in a career that interests them; flexibility is important, that is, a student interested in becoming an auto mechanic may have to settle for an article about someone in the auto industry.
3. The students complete the assigned worksheet.

NAME _____ PERIOD _____

DATE _____ **CAREER EXPLORATION**

Career being explored _____

Person chosen from *Current Biography* _____

Date of the yearbook _____

What was the person's training and/or education for this career?

_____

_____

_____

_____

What was the person's first job in this career?

_____

_____

What other jobs has he/she held in this career?

_____

_____

_____

What other jobs has he/she held outside this career?

_____

_____

_____

What makes this person outstanding in the work he/she is doing?

_____

_____

_____

_____

Unit: Conflict Resolution

Integrated Subject: Home Economics

Assignment

Students will read a novel that deals with topics related to conflict, friendship, family relationships, and communication, or a full-length biography of a peacemaker. Students will complete a written assignment based upon their reading.

Library Media Skills

- Learning that life lessons are dealt with in fiction and biography
- Selecting a novel or biography that deals with a specific subject
- Reading a novel or biography critically
- Writing about literature

Home Economics Curriculum Content

- Strengthening skills in conflict resolution through interpretive reading

Resources and Materials

- Novels dealing with interpersonal conflict, family relationships, peer relationships, friendship, communication, and so on
- Full-length biographies on the lives of peacemakers
- Assignment sheet

Activities

1. The library teacher selects novels and full-length biographies pertinent to the subject and places them on a cart or shelf for easy selection.
2. In the classroom, the teacher has been covering the principles and techniques of conflict resolution.
3. The library teacher explains the assignment and talks about at least one novel and one full-length biography that fit into the subject matter. Since students like mysteries and ghost stories, it is useful to point out that the conflict in the novel must exist between different people and not be a conflict of a person with something imagined or within himself or herself.
4. The library teacher and the classroom teacher assist students in selecting books.
5. When students are beginning to work on the written part of the assignment, the library teacher assists the classroom teacher in checking student progress. At this point, students may also work in peer writing groups.

Conflict Resolution: Assignment Sheet

If you read a **novel** dealing with conflict resolution, select one of the following questions for your written assignment:

1. Choose a character from the book and write a series of diary entries that this character may have written. Write them in the style of the character, and be sure that your entries deal with the issues of this unit.
2. Write an essay comparing and contrasting yourself with a character from the book. Concentrate on how you are alike and how you are different in dealing with conflict.
3. Write a series of letters between yourself and a character in the book. You and the character should share your ideas and thoughts about the conflict in the book.

If you read a **full-length biography** of a peacemaker, select one of the following questions for your written assignment:

1. Write an essay discussing the ways in which this person worked for peace.
2. Write a one-act play that highlights a significant event in the peacemaker's life.
3. Write a book for children that will put the person's life and accomplishments into a format understandable to a child from eight to ten years old.

MATHEMATICS

Unit: Careers in Mathematics

Integrated Subject: Mathematics

Assignment

After investigating three careers related to mathematics, the students select one of the three as chosen careers and give two reasons for their selection. Information gathered will be shared in a classroom discussion.

Library Media Skills
- Using the library catalog to locate career information
- Learning to use specific career related materials

Mathematics Curriculum Content
- Examining the necessity for mathematical skills in a variety of career choices
- Realizing that mathematics is an important part of adult life
- Sharing with classmates the role mathematics plays in the chosen career

Suggested Topics

Accountant	Floor Layer
Actuary	Salesperson
Aeronautical Technician	Hotel Manager
Air Traffic Controller	Industrial Designer
All-round Machinist	Instrument Mechanic
Architect	Investment Consultant
Architectural Technician	Landscape Architect
Astronomer	Mathematics Teacher
Auditor	Medical Technologist
Ballistics Expert	Optician
Bank Teller	Optometrist
Biochemist	Patternmaker
Cartographer	Pharmacist
Claim Adjuster	Pilot
Computer Programmer	Plumber
Computer Software Designer	Real Estate Broker
Construction Contractor	Sales Manager
Credit Manager	Surveyor
Economist	Tax Advisor
Electrician	Technical Illustrator
Engineer	Traffic Manager
FBI Agent	Trust Officer
	Underwriter

Resources and Materials
- *Dictionary of Occupational Titles*
- *Encyclopedia of Careers and Vocational Guidance*
- *Occupational Handbook*
- Occupational Outlook Handbook
  http://stats.bls.gov/ocohome.htm
- Pamphlet File Materials
- On-line Career Services
- Worksheet

Activities
1. The subject teacher introduces the activity and suggested careers. The students may select any related careers, the list offers suggestions only.
2. The library teacher identifies and explains the uses of available resources.
3. Using the library catalog, the students locate and use sources to research worksheet answers.
4. Using information gleaned in research, the students make a career choice and explain their reasons for the decision.
5. All students participate in a classroom roundtable.

NAME _____ PERIOD _____

DATE _____ **CAREERS IN MATHEMATICS**

Career: _____

Education Needed: _____

_____

_____

Mathematics Skills Used: _____

_____

_____

Nature of Work: _____

_____

_____

_____

Career: _____

Education Needed: _____

_____

_____

Mathematics Skills Used: _____

_____

_____

Nature of Work: _____

_____

_____

_____

Career: _____

Education Needed: _____

_____

_____

Mathematics Skills Used: _____

_____

_____

Nature of Work: _____

_____

_____

_____

Selected Career: _____

Reasons for Selection: (at least two) : _____

_____

_____

_____

_____

Unit: Census

Integrated Subject: Mathematics

Assignment

      Students will use the almanac and the Internet to gather statistics on the latest United States census. They will calculate percentages and make graphs by hand or with a computer.

Library Media Skills
- Using almanacs
- Using the Internet

Mathematics Curriculum Content
- Calculating percentages
- Graphing

Resources and Materials
- U.S. Bureau of the Census
  http://www.census.gov/
- Almanacs
- Worksheet
- Graph paper or computer graphing program

Activities
1. The classroom teacher instructs the class on calculating percentages and making graphs.
2. The library teacher instructs the class on reading charts in the almanac and using the Internet to locate specific information.
3. Students may work individually or in pairs. Each individual or pair is assigned a state on which statistical material will be gathered from the almanac and from the Internet. The name of the state is written on the top line of the worksheet.
4. Students gather the information and complete the worksheet with the assistance of the classroom teacher and the library teacher.
5. At the discretion of the classroom teacher, students may be instructed to group ages together before graphing.

NAME_____PERIOD_____

DATE_____**CENSUS**

State_____

Questions 1-3 are to be answered using an almanac.

    Title of almanac _____

1. Most recent population of the state_____

    Most recent population of the United States_____

    Percentage of U.S. population in this state_____

    Date of statistics_____

2. Name the three largest cities in the United States in the

    latest census, and write their populations. Calculate the

    percentage of the U.S. population that resides in each city.

City	Population	Percentage
_____	_____	_____
_____	_____	_____
_____	_____	_____

    Date of statistics_____

3. Number of immigrants to the United States who intend to reside

   in the state_____

   Total number of immigrants coming to the United States

   _____

   Percentage of the total number of immigrants who plan to

   settle in the state_____

   Date of statistics_____

4. Look up the population for your state on the Internet. List

   the number of people who live there according to their ages.

   Then, make a graph showing this population breakdown.

   WWW address_____

   0-4 years old_____

   5-9 years old_____

   10-13 years old_____

   14-17 years old_____

   18-24 years old_____

   25-34 years old_____

   35-44 years old_____

   45-54 years old_____

   55-59 years old_____

60-64 years old_____

65-74 years old_____

75-84 years old_____

85 and over_____

Date of statistics_____

MUSIC

Unit: Composers

Integrated Subject: Music

Assignment

Students will research the life, works, and impact of a composer, design a poster or record album cover including these important facts, and present to the class the visual product along with a sample of the composer's work. A bibliography of references is also handed in.

Library Media Skills

- Locating compact discs, cassette tapes, and records of the composer's work
- Locating information on the composer's life, work, and impact
- Scanning for information
- Taking notes
- Compiling a bibliography

Music Curriculum Content

- Listening to musical selection of famous composers
- Learning about the life of a composer and how the composer's work evolved
- Understanding the influence of various composers on the world of music

Resources and Materials

- *The Norton/Grove Dictionary of Women Composers*
- *International Encyclopedia of Women Composers*
- *Popular Composers*
- *American Composers Today*
- *Oxford Junior Companion to Music*
- *Milton Cross' Encyclopedia of Great Composers and Their Music*
- *Britannica Book of Music*
- *Composer Quest* (on compact disc)
- WWW Virtual Library Classical Music page
  http://www.gprep.pvt.k12.md.us/classical/index1.html
- Electronic encyclopedias
- Handout

Activities

1. The classroom teacher introduces students to the music of some great composers.
2. The library teacher reviews methods of locating information in print and electronic sources and methods of compiling a bibliography.
3. The library teacher and the classroom teacher assist the students in locating and synthesizing information.
4. Students select a musical passage that will be played during the oral presentation.
5. Students complete their album covers or posters as well as their bibliographies.

Composers: Handout

Thea Musgrave	Clara Schumann
Igor Stravinsky	Ludwig Beethoven
Arturo Toscanini	Johann Strauss
John Philip Sousa	Johannes Brahms
Leonard Bernstein	Richard Wagner
Francesca Caccini	Marianne Martinez
Aaron Copland	Fanny Mendelssohn
George Gershwin	Niccolo Paganini
Jacqueline Nova Sondag	Maria Prieto
W. C. Handy	Giacomo Puccini
Richard Rodgers	Gioacchino Rossini
Kay Swift	Betsy Jolas
Frederick Chopin	Giuseppe Verdi
Wolfgang Mozart	Edward Grieg
Franz Schubert	Nikolai Rimsky-Korsakov
Louis Berlioz	Peter Tchaikovsky
Georges Bizet	Sergei Rachmaninov
Claude Debussy	Felix Mendelssohn
Maurice Ravel	Gian Carlo Menotti
Johann Bach	Bela Bartok
Amy Beach	

Unit: What's That You're Hearing?

Integrated Subject: Music

Assignment

The students select five sound-producing objects and complete an information sheet concerning them.

Library Media Skills

- Using indexes effectively
- Becoming familiar with different methods of indexing
- Skimming to locate information
- Choosing main thoughts and supporting details
- Noting sources

Music Curriculum Content

- Realizing that music is based on sound
- Becoming aware of the variety of sounds around us
- Learning the ways sounds are transmitted

Suggested Topics

Accordion	Amplifiers
Amplitude magnification (AM)	Barrel organs
Carillons	Bells
Brass instruments	Broadcasting
Calliope	Cassettes
Cello	Hearing aids
Electronic jamming devices	Frequency modulation (FM)
Guitars	Harmonicas
HiFi Systems	Horns
Juke boxes	Loudspeakers
Music boxes	Noise
Percussion instruments	Phonographs
Pianos	Player pianos
Radios	Recorders
Records	Sirens
Sound	Sound effect machines
Sound mixing	Sound proofing
Sound tracks	Sound waves
Stereo	Stringed instruments
Tape (magnetic)	Tape recorders
Tuning forks	Voice analysis
Woodwind instruments	

Resources and Materials
- *How It Works*
- *The Way Things Work* (in book and compact disc)
- *Encyclopedia of Science and Technology*
- *The New Book of Popular Science*
- Encyclopedias
- Materials concerning electronics

Activities
1. Each topic is written on a card and placed in a fishbowl.
2. The library teacher explains the uses of the references, stressing their indexes.
3. The students select one topic, complete the worksheet on that topic, and select another until five topics are completed.

Suggestions
A science class studying sound could use this unit.

NAME _____ PERIOD _____

DATE _____ **WHAT'S THAT YOU'RE HEARING?**

For each of the sound-producing topics you choose from the fishbowl, provide the following information:
1. definition of term
2. brief description of how it works
3. source from which you take you information

TOPIC #1 _____

Definition_____

_____

Description of how it works_____

_____

_____

Source_____

◆◆◆

TOPIC #2 _____

Definition_____

_____

Description of how it works_____

_____

_____

Source_____

◆◆◆

TOPIC #3 _____

Definition_____

_____

Description of how it works_____

_____

_____

Source_____

◆◆

TOPIC #4 _____

Definition_____

_____

Description of how it works_____

_____

_____

Source_____

◆◆

TOPIC #5 _____

Definition_____

_____

Description of how it works_____

_____

_____

Source_____

PHYSICAL EDUCATION

Unit: The Olympics

Integrated Subject: Physical Education

Assignment

Students will locate materials relating to the Olympic Games, write bibliographic entries, and complete a worksheet.

Library Media Skills
- Selecting appropriate materials
- Synthesizing relevant information
- Writing bibliographic entries from various sources

Physical Education Curriculum Content
- Learning about outstanding athletes
- Referencing tools useful in physical education study

Resources and Materials
- *Webster's New Geographical Dictionary*
- *McGraw-Hill Encyclopedia of World Biography*
- *Famous First Facts*
- Yahoo's Olympic links
  http://www.yahoo.com/Recreation/Sports/Events/International_Games/
  Olympic_Games/
- Encyclopedias
- Atlases
- Almanacs
- Bibliography style sheet
- Library catalog
- Worksheet

Activities
1. The physical education teacher will discuss Olympic champions and their achievements.
2. The library teacher explains the location and use of source materials.
3. The library teacher distributes bibliographic style sheet and demonstrates its use.
4. The students complete worksheet.
5. The physical education teacher grades worksheets.

NAME _____ PERIOD _____

DATE _____ **THE OLYMPICS**

Answer these questions about the Olympic Games and write a bibliographic entry for each source using the appropriate form.

I. The library catalog

    A.   Name one of the books about the Olympics written by (author).

        _____

    B.   Write a bibliographic entry for the book.

        _____

        _____

        _____

II. Encyclopedias

    A.   Using an encyclopedia in electronic or book form, answer the following questions:

        1.   What do the five rings stand for?

            _____

        2.   What is the Olympic motto and what does it mean?

            _____

            _____

            _____

        3.   Where does the fire originate that is used to light the Olympic torch?

            _____

B.   Write a bibliographic entry (form for an electronic or book encyclopedia).

_____

_____

_____

III.   Geographic references

A.   Using *Webster's New Geographic Dictionary*, write three facts about (host city).

_____

_____

_____

B.   Write bibliographic entry (form starting with title).

_____

_____

_____

C.   Using an atlas, locate (host city) and your city. Place them on the world map included with this worksheet.

D.   Write bibliography entry (book form).

_____

_____

_____

IV.   Biographical references

A.   Using the *McGraw-Hill Encyclopedia of World Biography*, answer the following questions about Olympic hero, Jesse Owens.
        1.   Where was he born?

_____

2.   What record did he set?

_____

3.   In what year did he go to the Olympics?

_____

4.   Where were the games held that year?

_____

B.   Write a bibliographic entry (encyclopedia form)

_____

_____

_____

V.   References for unusual facts and statistics

A.   Using *Famous First Facts*, look up Olympic Games to find these little known facts.
1.   Who was the first American athlete to win ten games in the Olympics?

_____

2.   Who was the first American athlete to win four medals in one year?

_____

3.   Where was the first Olympic celebration in the United States held?

_____

B.   Write a bibliographic entry (book form).

_____

_____

_____

VI. Almanacs
   A. Using an almanac, find out who won each of the following events and where the winner came from.

   1. 1960 men's javelin throw

   _____

   2. 1984 women's 200 meter run

   _____

   3. 1920 men's hurdles — 110 meter

   _____

   4. 1992 middleweight boxing

   _____

   5. 1988 women's giant slalom

   _____

   6. 1984 Greco-Roman wrestling, over 200 pounds

   _____

   7. 1968 women's singles luge

   _____

   8. 1976 men's downhill skiing

   _____

   9. 1994 women's 500 meter speed skating

   _____

   10. 1972 men's figure skating

   _____

B.   Write a bibliographic entry (edited book form).

_____

_____

_____

VII.   The Internet.

    A.   Using Yahoo's Olympic link given in resources and materials, answer the following questions.

       1.   Where was the 1998 winter games held?

            _____

       2.   What was the permanent site of the ancient games?

            _____

       3.   How long was the course for the chariot races in the ancient games?

            _____

       4.   In what sport did Mark Spitz compete?

            _____

    B.   Write a bibliographic entry for the web site.

_____

_____

Olympics: Answer Sheet

II. A. 1. the five major cities
         2. "Citius, Altius, Fortius"
         3. Olympia Greece

IV. A. 1. Oakville, Alabama
         2. September12, 1913
         3. 1936
         4. Berlin
         5. 4 gold

V.   A. 1. Victor Tsibulenko, USSR
         2. Valerie Brisco-Hooks, United States
         3. Earl Thomson, Canada

VI. A. 1. Ariel Hernandez, Cuba
         2. Vreni Schneider, Switzerland
         3. Jeff Blatnik, United States
         4. Erica Lechner, Italy
         5. Franz Klammer, Austria
         6. Bonnie Blair, United States
         7. Ondrej Nepela, Czechoslovakia

VII. A. 1. Nagano, Japan
         2. Olympia
         3. 12 laps in the ancient stadium or 9 miles
         4. swimming

Unit: Sport Investigation

Integrated Subject: Physical Education

Assignment

After investigating a particular sport, each student will write an expository composition explaining the effect the sport had on him/her personally and the sport scene in general.

Library Media Skills
- Locating and using specific reference sources
- Notetaking
- Synthesizing information

Physical Education Curriculum Content
- Developing a knowledge of physical education reference sources
- Investigating a specific sport with particular reference to its history, method of play, and a famous player

Suggested Topics

Badminton	Baseball
Basketball	Bowling
Boxing	Fencing
Field Hockey	Football
Golf	Gymnastics
Handball	Ice Hockey
Karate	Lacrosse
Rollerblading	Rowing
Rugby	Skateboarding
Skydiving	Skiing
Soccer	Softball
Surfing	Swimming
Table Tennis	Tennis
Track and Field	Volleyball
Water Skiing	Weightlifting
Wrestling	Yachting

Resources and Materials
- *Encyclopedia of Sports*
- *Rand McNallly Encyclopedia of Sports*
- *Official Encyclopedia of Sports*
- *Oxford Companion to World Sports and Games*
- *Great Athletes: The Twentieth Century*

- Yahoo's lists of sports
  http://www.yahoo.com/Recreation/Sports/
- General encyclopedias (in book and compact disc forms)

Activities

1. After a brief explanation of the assignment and an introduction to the resources, students choose a sport and research it taking notes.
2. Using information from notes, student write the composition.

Unit: Sports Personalities

Integrated Subject: Physical Education

Assignment

    After learning the specific features of *Current Biography*, students will select a sports figure by using the "Classification by Profession" section. Student will read, take notes, and write a brief summary of the article.

Library Media Skills
- Notetaking from an oral presentation
- Learning about biographical tools in general and the specific purposes and features of *Current Biography*

Physical Education Curriculum Content
- Learning about a chosen sports figure

Resources and Materials
- *Current Biography*
- Worksheet for notetaking during presentation by library teacher

Activities
1. The library teacher instructs in the use and specific features of biographical references and specifically *Current Biography*.
2. The students take notes on the form provided.
3. After a brief explanation of the assignment, students select a sports figure, read, take notes on their own paper, and write a brief summary.

NAME _____ PERIOD _____

DATE _____ **SPORTS PERSONALITIES**

CURRENT BIOGRAPHY

Biographical References _____

_____

_____

Current Biography _____

_____

_____

_____

Special Features

List	Explanation
_____	_____
	_____
_____	_____
	_____
_____	_____
	_____
_____	_____
	_____

READING

Unit: Biography Book Talks

Assignment

Students will select a full-length biography to read and will prepare and deliver a biography book talk that is made up of clues about their subjects.

Library Media Skills

- Selecting a full-length biography
- Selecting interesting clues about the individual
- Organizing a book talk
- Presenting a book talk to the class

Resources and Materials

- Sheet of clues on famous people
- Full-length biographies

Activities

1. The library teacher locates unusual and interesting information and prepares clues from the biographies in the collection, arranging the clues in order of the most obscure to the most obvious.
2. The library teacher reads the clues one by one. Students attempt to guess the person with as few clues as possible.
3. The library teacher instructs the students to keep a list of possible clues and page numbers handy when they read, so that selecting the clues will be easier.
4. Students select and read a biography.
5. The library teacher and the classroom teacher assist the students in writing their clues and arranging them in order of most obscure to most obvious.
6. Students read their clues and try to get their classmates to discuss the identities of the subjects.

Suggestions

The clues provided here pertain to individuals whose biographies are in most collections. Students particularly enjoy it when the subjects are people they admire, so the addition of contemporary individuals is recommended.

Clues for Biography Book Talks

Subject: Laura Ingalls Wilder

She was born in Wisconsin on February 7, 1867.

When her older sister complained that she was a tomboy, she agreed. Only one boy in school could throw faster than she could, but he couldn't do it all of the time.

Her family moved west with the frontier and endured many hardships. When her sister went blind, she had to take on more responsibility at home.

The boy who would eventually become her husband first noticed her at a revival meeting and asked to take her home. She married Almonzo in 1885.

She became a teacher.

She began writing a book for children based on stories her father told her. The book was called *Little House in the Big Woods*.

She wrote several other books about her childhood including *Little House on the Prairie*.

Subject: Harry Houdini

His family came from Hungary, and he was the first child from the family to be born in this country.

His real name was Erich Weisz.

When boys his age were playing or trying to earn some money, he was practicing swimming, track, and breath control.

He learned to throw his shoulders out of joint, walk a tightrope, and untie knots with his teeth.

As an adult, he could make elephants disappear, get out of a 6-foot grave with his hands chained together, and remain under water longer than any human being known.

Subject: Theodore Roosevelt

The mother of this boy was horrified when the smell of dead fish was coming from her son's room where she found such things as an animal skin, a bird wing, and a snake that had been dead for weeks. He objected to her destroying his museum.

He was a sickly child suffering from asthma. He was always walking into and stumbling over things until his parents realized that his eyesight was very poor. Therefore, in all the pictures of him, he is wearing glasses.

He grew into an active and robust man who worked on his own ranch and led the Rough Riders in driving the Spaniards out of Cuba.

He became president of the United States when McKinley was assassinated.

Subject: Sojourner Truth

She was born in 1797. Her name at birth was Isabella Van Wagener.

For the first twenty-eight years of her life, she was a slave. When she became free, she renamed herself.

She and her parents lived in the cellar of the mansion with nine other slaves.

When she was eleven, her owner died. Her family was separated, and she was sold with a flock of sheep for one hundred dollars.

She sued to get her son back after he was sold into slavery in Alabama. She was one of the first Black women to win a court case, and her son was returned to her.

When she was forty-six years old, she began to speak publicly for the rights of Blacks and women. She was in great demand as a sincere and powerful speaker.

Unit: Readers' Forum

Assignment

Students will read books of their own choice and meet with the library teacher in small forums to discuss their reading.

Library Media Skills

- Furthering an appreciation of reading
- Sharing impressions of reading with peers

Resources and Materials

- Guide sheet of discussion questions

Activities

1. After students have finished reading books of their own choice, the classroom teacher divides them into groups of ten to twelve students for forum discussions in the library.
2. If possible, the library teacher should arrange that the forum be held in an informal setting with everyone sitting in a circle.
3. The library teacher explains that while this is an informal sharing and students need not raise their hands before speaking, the cardinal rule governing the discussion is that everyone must listen carefully to the person speaking and make comments or raise questions only when the speaker is finished.
4. The library teacher uses the sheet of discussion questions going in a round-robin fashion around the circle with each question.

Suggestions

This format of a Readers' Forum can be the cornerstone of the library's reading enrichment activities. It can be used with English teachers who incorporate a reading program into their curriculum. It can be used as a format for a reading club. Finally, it can be used in a Books for Lunch activity in which students eat their lunches while they discuss books.

The guide sheet suggests general questions that are applicable in most situations. However, the library teacher must be flexible so that there is a logical flow to the discussion. For example, if it is obvious that students have read the same book, books by the same author, or books on the same topic, lead questions may differ. Also, the round-robin format may be altered.

Readers' Forum—Discussion Questions

While the library teacher has to be flexible so that each forum can develop its own character, the following questions will be applicable to most discussions and are good places to begin:

1. Identify your book with a title, author, and brief summary.

2. Think about the characters of your book:
    -Who are the main characters?
    -How do they interact with each other?
    -What are the crises in their lives?
    -What decisions do they have to make? Do you agree with these decisions?
    -Are the characters realistic or true to life?
    -Would you want the characters as friends? Why?

3. What is the theme of your book? Is it relevant for today?

4. How would you characterize the style of the book? Think about the author's choice of words, use of description, and language.

5. Would you recommend the book? Why or why not?

6. Would you read other books by the same author?

7. Have you become interested in reading any of the books discussed by other students today?

Unit: Book Reviews on Disc

Assignment

Students will enter book reviews into a computer database.

Library Media Skills
- Reading critically
- Selecting details to include in a book review
- Entering data in a database

Resources and Materials
- Form on which students write their database entry
- Database program

Activities
1. The library teacher creates a database to include author, title, call number, type of book, brief summary, and evaluation.
2. The library teacher leads the class in a discussion of what kind of books they like and what makes a book interesting—characters, plot, suspense, fantasy, and so on. They also talk about how they select a book to read; one of the methods is undoubtedly recommendation of other students. This will lead the discussion into the use of a database as a means for students to recommend books to their peers.
3. The library teacher explains the form on which students will write the information that will be put into the database.
4. The library teacher demonstrates the inputting of data into the database.
5. The recommendations are stored on the hard drive for students to refer to when selecting books.

NAME_____PERIOD_____

DATE_____**BOOK REVIEWS ON DISC**

Supply the following information for the book you are reviewing.
Have this paper approved by your library teacher or your classroom
teacher before putting the information into the database.

Author_____

Title_____

Call number_____

Type of book (mystery, science fiction, etc.)_____

Summary_____

_____

_____

_____

_____

Evaluation_____

_____

_____

_____

_____

_____

Library teacher\classroom teacher signature_____

SCIENCE

Unit: Classification of Organisms

Integrated Subject: Science

Assignment

Students will use library resources to classify and describe organisms used by the Indians of the region. The students will generate a bibliography for all sources used.

Library Media Skills
- Practicing using indexes
- Learning the uses and the presentations of several scientific references

Science Curriculum Content
- Identifying organisms by common and scientific names
- Learning the description, habitat, and feeding habits of each
- Becoming knowledgeable of some of the library's resources in the science field

Resources and Materials
- *International Wildlife Encyclopedia*
- *Macmillan Illustrated Science Encyclopedia*
- *Encyclopedia of Reptiles and Amphibians*
- *Animal Atlas of the World*
- *Oxford Encyclopedia Trees of the World*
- *Wildflowers*
- *The North American Indian*
- *The World of American Indians*
- *Indians of the Longhouse*
- Field guides and handbooks
- Electronic resources where available

Activities
1. The science teacher hands out worksheets and explains the expected outcomes.
2. The library teacher presents materials and their uses.
3. The library teacher presents or reviews bibliographic techniques.

Suggestions

This is a perfect opportunity for a disciplinary interaction with social studies during the study of Indian culture. Home state may be substituted for New York and regional sources added.

Directions: Select an organism from each of the three categories, create a bibliography on the bibliography page, and investigate the following details of each organism you selected.

MEAT AND FISH		**FARM PRODUCTS**	**FOREST PRODUCTS**	
deer	squirrel	corn	chestnuts	hickory nuts
black bear	otter	squash	butternuts	hazelnuts
beaver	pigeon	beans	acorns	strawberries
raccoon	grouse	sunflower	blackberries	blueberries
wild turkey	crayfish	tobacco	cranberries	groundnuts
wolf	clams	pumpkins	turnips	pond lily
lynx	turtles		plums	cherries
fox	frogs		wild leeks	wild garlic
porcupine	ducks		grapes	mushrooms
rabbit			apples	roots

MEAT AND FISH

Common name _____ Scientific name _____

Locations found _____

Physical description _____

_____

_____

Habitat _____

_____

Feeding habits _____

How used by Indians _____

_____

FARM PRODUCTS

Common name _____   Scientific name _____

Physical description _____

_____

Growth season _____

How used by Indians _____

_____

FOREST PRODUCTS

Common name _____   Scientific name _____

Physical description _____

_____

Location in New York _____

Growth season _____

How used by Indians _____

_____

Unit: Science in the News

Integrated Subject: Science

Assignment

As an ongoing weekly assignment, the students locate, read, summarize and give a brief oral report on a science related newspaper or magazine article.

Library Media Skills
- Skimming to locate information
- Reading carefully to locate facts
- Selecting main thoughts and supporting details

Science Curriculum Content
- Locating periodical or newspaper articles pertaining to current happenings/discoveries in any field of science (life, earth, physical).

Resources and Materials
- Science Daily
  http://www.sciencedaily.com/
- Science News Online
  http://www.sciencenews.org/
- Discover magazine
  http://www.enews.com/magazines/discover/
- CNN Sci-Tech
  http://www.cnn.com/TECH/
- ABCNEWS.com Science
  http://www.abcnews.com/sections/science/index.html
- Periodicals, newspapers

Activities
1. The science teacher shows an example of an appropriate news article, written summary and oral report to the class.
2. The students use library and home resources to find articles and write summaries as a homework assignment.
3. Each week, selected students give oral reports.
4. Particularly interesting articles and summaries are posted on the bulletin board.

Suggestions

This is a good opportunity to encourage students to see the importance of science in the world in which they live and to discover the wide range of fields in which science is used. The students who find particularly exciting or interesting news articles could be given extra credits for their extra effort.

Unit: Chemical Element Report

Integrated Subject: Science

Assignment
Using a variety of reference materials, the students will investigate two elements and complete a fact sheet for each. The students will select one of the elements and create a mobile displaying the information discovered.

Library Media Skills
- Locating and using specific science reference sources
- Using book and electronic indexes with the stress on cross referencing and key word searches
- Compiling a working bibliography

Science Curriculum Content
- Answering questions about the history, properties, uses, and how the element is obtained from nature
- Completing a fact sheet for two elements and reporting this information

Resources and Materials
- General encyclopedias
- *New Junior Encyclopedia of Science*
- *New Book of Popular Science*
- *Concise Encyclopedia of the Sciences*
- *Harper Encyclopedia of Science*
- *Van Nostrand's Scientific Encyclopedia*
- *World Almanac*
- Web Elements
  http://www.shef.ac.uk/uni/academic/A-C/chem/web-elements/web-elements-home.html
- Chemicool Periodic Table
  http://the-tech.mit.edu/Chemicool/
- Web Elements
  http://chemserve.bc.edu/web-elements-home.html

Activities
1. The library teacher introduces appropriate sources and instructs on their uses.
2. The students locate and select references to find information on two elements — One common and one uncommon.
3. The students build a mobile displaying the information.

NAME _____ PERIOD _____

DATE _____ **CHEMICAL ELEMENTS REPORT**

Element's Name: _____

Original Name: _____

Symbol: _____ Metal _____ Metalloid _____ Nonmetal _____

Atomic Number: _____ Atomic Mass: _____

Draw Bohr Model:

History: _____

_____

_____

_____

_____

Physical Properties: _____

_____

_____

Chemical Properties: _____

_____

_____

_____

Uses: _____

_____

_____

_____

_____

_____

_____

How it is obtained from nature: _____

_____

_____

_____

_____

Books Used:

Author	Title	City	Publisher	Date

Make a mobile showing traits of the element.

Unit: Biography of a Scientist

Integrated Subject: Science

Assignment

    The students will use the library catalog and other specific reference sources to do biographical research on a scientist in order to write a biographical sketch.

Library Media Skills
- Using the library catalog
- Reading to obtain facts and taking notes on cards
- Synthesizing and paraphrasing information

Science Curriculum Content
- Learning specific library tools helpful in scientific research
- Investigating the life of an important scientist

Suggested Topics
- Students will select scientists from attached lists

Resources and Materials
- Library catalog
- *Concise Dictionary of American Biography*
- *Webster's American Biography*
- *Webster's Biographical Dictionary*
- *Scientists and Inventors*
- *Asimov's Biographical Encyclopedia of Science and Technology*
- *McGraw Hill Encyclopedia of World Biography*
- *Concise Dictionary of Scientific Biography*
- *Notable American Women*
- *Current Biography*
- Yahoo's List of Scientists
  http://www.yahoo.com/Arts/Humanities/History/Science_and_Technology/People/
- 4000 Year of Women in Science
  http://crux.astr.ua.edu/4000WS/4000WS.html
- Treasure Trove of Scientific Biography
  http://www.astro.virginia.edu/~eww6n/bios/bios.html
- MacTutor History of Mathematics — Index of biographies
  http://www.groups.mcs.st-and.ac.uk/~history/BioIndex.html

Activities
1. Students locate specific information about their scientist.
2. Students write a biographical sketch covering the following points:
   Where and when did the person live, work, and die?
   How did this person contribute to science and technology?

What things (family, people, education, money, previous discoveries, etc.) influenced his/her career?

Was anything going on in the world at the same time(wars, inventions) that made a difference in the person's life?

Which branch(es) of science benefited most from this person's work?

3.   Each sketch must be accompanied with a proper bibliography.

Scientists

Andre Ampere
Joselyn Elders
Henri Becquerel
Nicolaus Copernicus
Gertrude Elion
George Washington Carver
John Dalton
Christian Doppler
John Priestley
Jane Goodall
Albert Einstein
Annie Jump Cannon
Enrico Fermi
Galileo Galilei
George Gamov
Werner Heisenberg
Carl Sagan
Christian Huygens
Gregor Mendel
Jonas Salk
E. O. Lawrence
Edwin Hubble
Dmitri Mendeleev
Florence Sabin
Rosalyn Yalow
Dorothy Hodgkin

Linus Pauling
Anders Angstrom
Maria Mayer
William Herschel
Marie Curie
Niels Bohr
Dian Fossey
Lise Mietner
Erwin Schroedinger
Ernest Rutherford
Rene Decartes
Michael Faraday
Williamina Fleming
Charles Goodyear
Edmond Halley
Joseph Henry
Robert Koch
James Jaule
Albert Sabin
Joseph Hooker
Robert Boyle
Barbara McClintock
Karl Jansky
George Ohm
Harold Urey
Robert Oppenheimer

Unit: Experiment

Integrated Subject: Science

Assignment

    The students will locate, replicate, and write up a science experiment. The experiment must be stated in the following manner: Problem, Materials, Method, Results, and Conclusions.

Library Media Skills
- Locating and using library resources
- Stating source in correct bibliographic form

Science Curriculum Content
- Reporting information according to scientific method

Resources and Materials
- *Nature Projects for Young Scientists*
- *Background Scientist Series Two and Four*
- *Science Experiments You Can Eat*
- *Science in Your Backyard*
- *Projects in Space Science*
- *Space Projects for Young Scientists*
- *Experimenting with Light*
- *Experiments with Light and Illusions*
- *Investigate and Discover Light*
- *Experiment with Light and Mirrors*
- *Experiments with Motion*
- *Experimenting with Sound*
- *Designs in Science*
    Using Light
    Materials Using Sound
    Water
    Using Energy
    Movement
- *Everyday Material Science Experiments*
    Force and Energy
    Air and Gases
    Salts and Solids
    Water and Other Liquids
    Plastics and Polymers
- *Experimenting with Plants*
- *Experimenting with a Microscope*
- *Exploring with the Microscope*
- *Investigating Nature Through Outdoor Projects*
- *Science Projects about Chemistry*

- *Experimenting with Surface Tension and Bubbles*
- *Astronomy Activity Book*
- The Science Club
  http://www.halcyon.com/sciclub/
- Newton's Apple
  http://ericir.syr.edu/Projects/Newton/
- Franklin Institute
  http://sln.fi.edu/qanda/spotlight1/spotlight1.html

Activities

1. The students are introduced to scientific method by the science teacher .
2. The science teacher introduces and explains the assignment.
3. The library teacher introduces sources.
4. The students select an experiment, write down the materials needed to do the experiment, and get permission to do it.
5. The students perform the experiment at home and write it up in the manner prescribed.
6. The students include a bibliography with the write-up.
7. The students orally describe the procedures followed to the class.

Suggestions

It is essential that the science teacher review each experiment to make sure that no dangerous materials or methods are involved.

Unit: Scientific Classification

Integrated Subject: Science

Assignment

Students will scavenger hunt in the library to locate the genus and species of selected plants and animals.

Library Media Skills

- Using library catalog and book indexes

Science Curriculum Content

- Locating materials useful for scientific research
- Identifying the genus and species for thirty organisms

Resources and Materials

- *Animals Without Backbones*
- *Oxford Encyclopedia Trees of the World*
- *Reader's Digest North American Wildlife*
- *International Wildlife Encyclopedia*
- *Encyclopedia of Reptiles and Amphibians*
- *Wild Flowers*
- Animal Bytes Database
  http://www.seaworld/animal_bytes/animal_bytes.html
- Other appropriate science materials

Activities

1. The science teacher introduces and teaches the system of plant and animal classification to students.
2. Students have a scavenger hunt in the library to identify thirty organisms.

SCAVENGER HUNT

Find the genus and species name for each organism below.

Organism	Genus	Species
1. Amoeba		
2. Paramecium		
3. Bear (Grizzly)		
4. Dog		
5. Panther		
6. Chimpanzee		
7. Manta ray		
8. Manatee		
9. Elm tree		
10. Whippoorwill		
11. Caribou		
12. Bread mold		
13. Black-eyed Susan		
14. Horse		
15. Porcupine		
16. Earthworm		
17. Pines (Scotch)		
18. Geranium		

19. Rattlesnake (Timber)   _____   _____

20. Bacterium (Pneumonia causing)   _____   _____

21. Bald Eagle   _____   _____

22. Coyote   _____   _____

23. White oak   _____   _____

24. Cobra (Indian)   _____   _____

25. Grass frog   _____   _____

26. Robin (European)   _____   _____

27. Mosquito   _____   _____

28. Bat (Vampire)   _____   _____

29. Road runner   _____   _____

30. Venus flytrap   _____   _____

Scientific Classification: Answers

1. *Amoeba proteus*
2. *Paramecium caudatum*
3. *Ursus horribilis*
4. *Canis familiaris*
5. *Panthera pardus*
6. *Pan troglodytes*
7. *Manta birostris*
8. *Trichechus manatus*
9. *Ulmus americana*
10. *Caprimulgus vociferus*
11. *Rangifer tarandus articus*
12. *Rhizopus nigricans*
13. *Rudbeckia hirta*
14. *Equus cabullus przewalskii*
15. *Erithizon dorsatum*
16. *Lumbricus terrestris*
17. *Pinus sylvestris*
18. *Geranium maculatum*
19. *Crotalus horridus*
20. *Diplococcus pneumonia*
21. *Haliaeetus leucocephalus*
22. *Canis latrans*
23. *Quercus alba*
24. *Naja naja*
25. *Rana temporaria*
26. *Erithacus rubecula*
27. *Culex pipiens*
28. *Diaemus youngi*
29. *Geococcyx californianus*
30. *Dionaea muscipula*

Unit: Physical Science Research

Integrated Subject: Science

Assignment

    Students will prepare a written paper including a correct bibliography on one of the physical science topics listed. In addition, students will give an oral presentation to summarize their findings. Each presentation must be accompanied by a visual.

Library Media Skills
- Locating and using a variety of reference sources
- Selecting and verifying a research topic
- Finding needed information
- Compiling a working bibliography
- Notetaking
- Report writing including a correct bibliography

Science Curriculum Content
- Locating library materials pertinent to a physical science principle or principles
- Finding information to write a science report pertaining to these principles

Suggested Topics

LIGHT
    fiber optics
    lasers
    cameras
    photography
    rainbows
    colors
    mirages
    optical illusions

CHEMISTRY
    acid rain

MAGNETISM
    superconductors

COMPUTERS
    electronic chips

SOUND
    sonar
    musical instruments
    ultrasound
    waves
    noise pollution

SOLAR ENERGY
    house plans
    solar collector
    active vs. passive

ELECTRICITY
    light bulb
    house circuitry
    lightning (static electricity)

Resources and Materials
- *Concise Encyclopedia of Science*
- *Harper Encyclopedia of Science*
- *Van Nostrand's Scientific Encyclopedia*
- *New Book of Popular Science*
- Magazine indexes (in book and compact disc form)
- Encyclopedias (in book and compact disc form)

Activities
1. The science teacher introduces students to the physics unit of study by a presentation of the topics listed.
2. Students select topic for their research projects, check library sources for information, and prepare a working bibliography as they progress. Each project will include at least a three - page written report, a cover page, and a bibliography with at least three sources. Only one source may be from a general encyclopedia.
3. Along with the written report, students will prepare a visual to illustrate a principle from the project. This may be a graph, poster, model, or other teacher-approved visual.
4. Students give a short oral report to the class, summarizing findings, and displaying and explaining the visual.

Unit: Energy — Critical Thinking

Integrated Subject: Science

Assignment

   Students investigate the varied aspects of present and future energy resources. Using current materials, students find how the energy is captured, how it is used, what are the energy transfers that are involved in the production and use, and what the positive and negative effects are on the environment. Students will draw conclusions from these findings and formulate an argument either for or against the use of this form of energy. Students will prepare a ten-minute presentation to the class. Students must be prepared to defend their position when questioned by the class.

Library Media Skills
   - Locating and selecting appropriate materials
   - Using magazine indexes in book and electronic form
   - Using *Social Issues and Resources Series* in print and electronic form

Science Curriculum Content
   - Exploring present and future energy sources
   - Using scientific data to form a conclusion

Suggested Topics
   Solar power
   Oil
   Hydropower
   Biomass energy
   Geothermal energy
   Nuclear power

Resources and Materials
   - *SIRS* in book and electronic form
   - Magazine indexes in book and electronic form
   - Yahoo's Energy Site
     www.yahoo.com/Science/Energy
   - Current books on the topic

Activities
   1. Students receive an explanation of the assignment by the classroom teacher.
   2. Library teacher explains the availability and use of library resources in the study of power resources.
   3. Students find and read information concerning their selected form of energy and prepare a ten-minute oral presentation.
   4. Students present findings and conclusions to the class.

Unit: Plant Organism Collection Project

Integrated Subject: Science

Assignment

    After collecting five plant organisms from their neighborhood environment, the students will use library resources to identify and to learn appropriate methods of preserving them. Students will compile a bibliography to identify sources used.

Library Media Skills
- Locating nature field guides and other pertinent materials by using the library catalog
- Studying illustrations in scientific materials to identify plant organisms
- Compiling a bibliography

Science Curriculum Content
- Participating in a nature walk
- Collecting plant organisms
- Identifying common and scientific name (genus and species) for each
- Using proper methods (drying, waxing, sealing, etc.) to preserve materials

Resources and Materials
- Plant Encyclopedia
  http://www.gardening.com/Encyclopedia/Default.htm
- Botany Classification
  http://www.mancol.edu/science/biology/plants_new/intro.plntlist.html
- Nature field guides
- Science materials

Activities
1. The subject teacher takes students on a nature walk to motivate and clarify types of organisms to be collected.
2. The students go to their own neighborhoods to collect five different specimens from the environment. Organisms must be from the same group (five leaves, five seeds, etc.).
3. Using library resources, the students identify organisms.
4. The students preserve items and mount them on a background of their choice.
5. The students compile a bibliography.

Unit: Animal Investigation

Integrated Subject: Science

Assignment

The student will select "a critter" from any animal class: Mammalia, reptilia, and so on, locate materials, and design a poster illustrating the facts from each of the five categories.

Library Media Skills
- Using library catalog to locate source
- Using science print and electronic materials

Science Curriculum Content
- Locating materials for use with the science curriculum
- Learning about a specific animal
- Creating a poster to report about the animal

Resources and Materials
- *North American Wildlife*
- *Parade of the Animal Kingdom*
- *International Wildlife Encyclopedia*
- *Larousse Encyclopedia of Animal Life*
- *Pictorial Encyclopedia of Insects*
- *Birds of America*
- *Imperial Collection of Audubon Animals*
- *Animal Atlas of the World*
- *National Geographic Book of Mammals* (book and CD)
- *Macmillan Illustrated Science Encyclopedia*
- *Encyclopedia of Insects*
- *Oxford Book of Invertebrates*
- *Encyclopedia of Reptiles and Amphibians*

Activities
1. The science teacher gives students specific instruction in the techniques of organizing and completing this project.
2. The students are directed to sources and given a brief explanation of their contents and use.
3. Additional materials are located through using the library catalog.
4. The students locate least three sources.
5. The students create posters using original drawings or cut-out pictures. Notes and bibliography are handed in with posters.

Animal Investigation: Handout

1. Select "a critter" from any animal class: Mammalia, Reptilia, and so on.

2. Set up note cards to obtain information on the following categories:
   a. Life cycle
   b. Niche/habitat
   c. Biome
   d. Geographical distribution
   e. Place in the food web

3. Fill out source cards for at least three resources. Be sure to include the correct information for a bibliographic entry for each resource. For example, a source card for a book would include author, title, city, publisher, and copyright date.

4. Gather complete and accurate information for each category. Include all information on your note cards.

5. Design a poster using your own creativity to illustrate the facts. The poster should be done on large construction paper or oaktag. All lettering must be neat and legible from a distance. Each of the five categories from #2 must be included in the design.

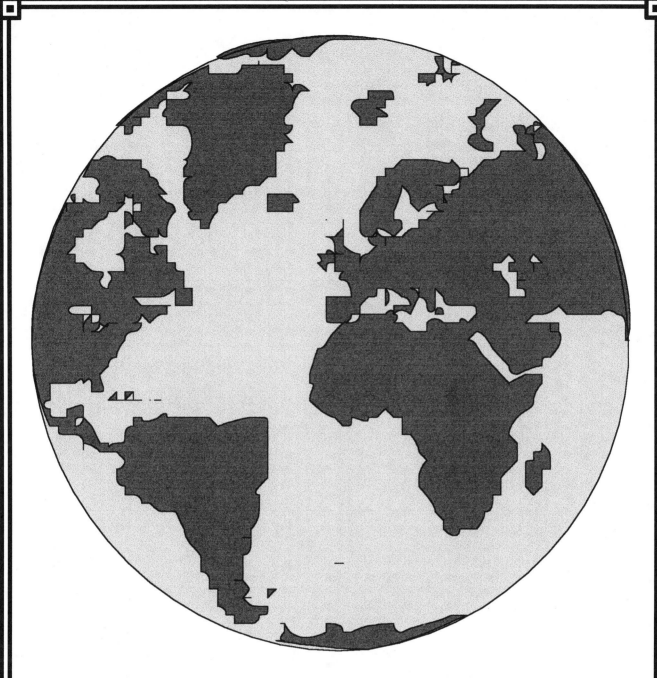

SOCIAL STUDIES

Unit: Introduction to Report Writing / Explorers

Integrated Subject: Social Studies

Assignment

Based upon library research and using prescribed procedures, the students will write a report about the assigned explorer. Each report must include a title page, a report of at least two pages, a map, and a bibliography.

Library Media Skills

- Selecting appropriate sources and prepare a working bibliography
- Notetaking in a prescribed manner
- Reading for information
- Synthesizing data and organizing material
- Writing a report including a bibliography

Social Studies Curriculum Content

- Investigating the life of an explorer with emphasis on the reasons for and the historical impact of the exploration
- Developing skills in expository writing
- Locating and using sources relevant to the social studies curriculum

Suggested Topics: Explorers

Columbus	Balboa
daGama	Ponce de Leon
Prince Henry — Portugal	Estevanico
Cartier	Cortez
Champlain	Pizarro
LaSalle	Coronado
Magellan	de Soto
Hudson	Sir Francis Drake
Marquette	Dias
Verrazano	Cabeza de Vaca
Frobisher	Vespucci
Joliet	Cabrillo
Cabot	Cook

Resources and Materials

- *McGraw-Hill Encyclopedia of World Biography*
- *Webster's Biographical Dictionary*
- *Shepard's Historical Atlas*
- *The Discovers*
- All library resources relating to the historical period and the explorers
- Assessment sheet and handout

Activities

1. After the classroom teacher introduces the explorer unit, the library teacher introduces the assignment to the students, explaining the requirements, the time line, and the assessment process. Resources particularly useful to the research are presented.
2. Students prepare a working bibliography.
3. Using the section titled "what do you need to know?" on the handout <u>Report Writing Made Easy</u>, the library teacher demonstrates the proper technique of taking notes on cards. Idea label and source are indicated on every card.
4. Students practice taking notes from an encyclopedia article.
5. Students locate at least five sources, read for information, take notes, and complete written report.
6. The subject and library teachers grade all sections of the report.

NAME _____ PERIOD _____

DATE _____ **INTRODUCTION TO REPORT WRITING/EXPLORERS**

ASSESSMENT SHEET

	Possible Points	Your Points
Practice notetaking	5	_____
Library research work daily scale 3 - 0	15	_____
Notecards	20	_____
Outline	5	_____
Bibliography	15	_____
Cover page	5	_____
Map	5	_____
Paper	30	_____
		_____

Comment:

REPORT WRITING MADE EASY

1. Where do you begin?
    A. Write down your sources.
    B. Get the facts.
    C. Write them down in your own words.
    D. Check to see if you have all the information.

2. What do you need to know?
    A. Biographical information (when and where did the explorer live, was the explorer rich and influential or poor and struggling, what was important about the explorer?)
    B. Reasons for exploration (why did explorer go on the voyage, why did the country of origin finance the expedition — profit, territorial expansion, etc.)
    C. Historical impact of exploration (what was the result of the exploration, did it affect the people in the country of origin, did it change conditions in the country explored, did it have any effect on today's world?)

3. What are you trying to say?
    A. Organize your notes.
    B. Organize your thoughts; make an outline if it is easier for you.
    C. Read your notes — know your information.
    D. Write a summary statement — a brief description of what the reader should know after reading your paper.

4. How do you put the report into words?
    A. Introduction - In two or three sentences, tell the purpose of your paper.
    B. Body - Write one paragraph about each topic on your notecards.
    C. Conclusion - In two or three sentences, tell the reader what you have done.

REPORT FORMAT

Title Page
- ◆ Center title in middle of page.
- ◆ Lower left — your name and date

♦ Lower right — your teacher's name and social studies period

The Paper
♦ Write neatly.
♦ Write on front of paper only.
♦ Use complete sentences and paragraphs.

The map
♦ Neatly title map.
♦ Label important places.

Bibliography
♦ Must have at least three sources.
♦ Use specified form.

Unit: Social Studies References

Integrated Subject: Social Studies

Assignment

After a brief overview of the library's holdings of social studies reference books, the students will complete worksheets using specific social studies reference materials.

Library Media Skills
- Locating and using specific reference books

Social Studies Curriculum Content
- Reviewing skills needed to do social studies reference and research assignments
- Finding social studies information through the use of specific sources

Resources and Materials
- *Webster's Biographical Dictionary*
- *Concise Dictionary of American Biography*
- *Dictionary of American Biography*
- *McGraw-Hill Encyclopedia of World Biography*
- *Current Biography*
- *Webster's Geographical Dictionary*
- *Historical Atlas*
- *Concise Dictionary of American History*
- *Dictionary of American History*
- *The Encyclopedia of American Facts and Dates*
- *Encyclopedia of American History*
- Worksheet
- Fact sheet

Activities
1. The library teacher will present fact sheet demonstrating the format and uses of each social studies reference book.
2. The student will locate books in the library and use them to complete the worksheet.

Social Studies References

Reference materials that are specifically helpful in the social studies area include information about people, places, and events. These include almanacs, atlases, and biographical and historical references. The following is a brief outline and description of some of these references that appear in the library.

1. ***Webster's Biographical Dictionary***
   a) brief entries
   b) good starting point

2. ***Concise Dictionary of American Biography***
   a) concise biographies
   b) entries based on the lengthy articles in <u>Dictionary of American Biography</u>

3. ***Dictionary of American Biography***
   a) no living persons included
   b) subject should have lived in United States territory
   c) subject should have made significant contribution to American life
   d) original volumes plus supplements

4. ***McGraw-Hill Encyclopedia of World Biography***
   a) five thousand articles
   b) alphabetical arrangement
   c) subjects are international in many areas of accomplishment

5. ***Current Biography***
   a) living leaders in all fields
   b) cumulative indexes
   c) dated arrangement

6. ***Webster's Geographical Dictionary***
   a) similar to ***Webster's Biographical Dictionary***
   b) brief entries on places
   c) pronunciation and concise geographical information

7. ***Historical Atlas***
   a) on volume supplying maps from the history of ancient Greece to modern times
   b) map keys supply essential information

8. *Concise Dictionary of American History*
   a) abridgment of *Dictionary of American History*
   b) essential information about events in American history from pre-Columbian times

9. *Dictionary of American History*
   a) alphabetical arrangement
   b) in-depth articles

10. *Encyclopedia of American Facts and Dates*
    a) four parallel columns; politics and government, etc., books, etc., science, etc., sports, etc.
    b) chronological order
    c) facts and events from American life

11. *Encyclopedia of American History*
    a) chronological arrangement basic chronology — politics and military
    b) topical chronology — economic, scientific, cultural

NAME _____ SOCIAL STUDIES PERIOD _____

DATE _____ **SOCIAL STUDIES REFERENCES**

Atlases and Geographical References

_____ 1. What is the copyright date of the *Rand McNally New International Atlas*?

_____ 2. What area of the United States is pictured in a map on pages 104-105 of the *World Book Atlas*?

3. *Webster's Geographical Dictionary*
_____ a. How high is Macomb Mountain?

_____ b. What is Katzenbuckel? What country is it in?

4. *Historical Atlas*
_____ On what page does a United States map showing slave and free states appear?

Biographical References

1. *Webster's Biographical Dictionary*
_____ a. In what year did Thomas Jefferson graduate from the College of William and Mary?

_____ b. Who was Alonso de Ojeda?

2. *McGraw-Hill Encyclopedia of World Biography*
_____ a. What is the arrangement of this encyclopedia?

_____ b. What is Elisha Otis famous for?

_____ c. Where did he move when he was 19?

3. *Dictionary of American Biography*
   a. What cause did Henry Berg work for?

   _____

   b. What was Thomas Nast's occupation?

   _____

4. *Current Biography*
   a. Whose biography begins on page 191 of the 1981 volume?

   _____

   b. How are the volumes labeled?

   _____

Historical References

1. *Dictionary of American History*
   a. What was the Great Massacre?

   _____

   b. The sow case grew out of a debate between two people on the ownership of a pig. Who are they?

   _____

2. *Encyclopedia of American Facts and Dates*
   a. The Loeb-Leopold trial is found under which column?

   _____

   b. In what year did the term "Black Power" originate?

   _____

3. *Encyclopedia of American History*
   a. What is the first chapter heading in Topical Chronology?

   _____

   b. In what year did William T. Sherman march through Georgia?

   _____

Social Studies References: Answers

Atlases and Geographical References

1. 1981
2. Northeast
3. (a) 4,371
    (b) Mountain; Germany
4. 206 -207

Biographical References

1. (a) 1762
    (b) Explorer with Columbus

2. (a) Alphabetical
    (b) Elevator
    (c) Troy, NY

3. (a) Animal protection — A.S.P.C.A.
    (b) Cartoonist

4. (a) Debbie Harry
    (b) with index from (date) to (date)

Historical References

1. (a) Indian attack in Virginia
    (b) Sherman and Keanye

2. (a) 1924 - IV
    (b) 1966

3. (a) Territorial expansion
    (b) 1864

Unit: The Forgotten Presidents

Integrated Subject: Social Studies

Assignment

Students will investigate the life of one of the lesser known presidents and create a campaign poster, a television ad promotion, or a campaign speech that demonstrates the information.

Library Media Skills
- Using specific biographical and historic references to locate information
- Taking effective notes
- Compiling a bibliography of at least two sources

Social Studies Curriculum Content
- Locating and using sources useful for social studies research
- Extracting information about the achievements of lesser known presidents
- Gathering information that is relevant but not necessarily stressed in social studies
- Creating a report that demonstrates this information

Resources and Materials
- *Encyclopedia of World Biography*
- *Dictionary of World Biography*
- *The Presidents: a Reference History*
- *Facts about the Presidents*
- *The Glorious Burden*
- *The Complete Book of Presidents*
- *Chronology of the United States*
- Grolier Online's The American Presidency
  http://www.grolier.com/presidents/preshome.html
- The President of the United States from The White House
  http://www1.whitehouse.gov/WH/glimpse/presidents/html/presidents.html
- Internet Public Library's POTUS
  http://www.ipl.org/ref/POTUS
- Yahoo's List of Presidents
  http://www.yahoo.com/Arts/Humanities/History/U_S__History/People/Presidents

Activities
1. The teacher explains the activity to the students having them brainstorm and record the names of the presidents that they know. These are eliminated from the master list of presidents. The students may choose a subject from the presidents remaining.

2. The students research presidential achievements with particular attention paid to those achieved prior to election (e.g., Ulysses S. Grant — General in the Union Army during the Civil War).
3. Following a discussion of campaign strategies and philosophies, students design projects to promote election or reelection. The projects must illustrate the historical achievements of the person.

NAME _____ PERIOD _____

DATE _____ **THE FORGOTTEN PRESIDENTS**

My president is _____

Dates of presidency _____ to _____

Number of presidency _____

Biographical Information _____

_____

_____

_____

_____

_____

_____

Historical Information _____

_____

_____

_____

_____

_____

_____

_____

Unit: Historical Fiction

Integrated Subject: Social Studies

Assignment

      Students will select and read a book in the historical fiction genre. During reading, students will keep a reading journal. Upon completion of the book, students will come to the library to do the related worksheet. Both the journal entries and the worksheet will be used as a basis of class or small group discussion.

Library Media Skills
- Identifying the elements of a specific literary genre
- Developing the habit of leisure reading
- Becoming a discriminating reader
- Writing a bibliography

Social Studies Curriculum Content
- Seeing that historical events are used as a basis for historical novels
- Checking the historical accuracy of the main event

Resources and Materials
- Historical fiction
- Encyclopedias
- History books
- Worksheet
- Reading journal

Activities
1. The library teacher explains the elements of historical fiction, by giving a book talk or merely citing examples.
2. The students select an historical fiction book.
3. The students read the book by the assigned date keeping a journal during the process.
4. The students complete the worksheet in the library.
5. The students take part in a discussion.

1. Write a bibliographic entry for the historical book you have read.

   _____

   _____

   _____

2. What historical event is the basis for the book?

   _____

3. When did this event take place?

   _____

4. What historical figures are characters in the book?

   _____

   _____

5. Use an encyclopedia or a history book to check the main facts about the event and answer the following questions:
   a) In what ways is the novel accurate in describing the event?

   _____

   _____

   _____

   b) In what ways is the novel inaccurate in describing the event?

   _____

   _____

   _____

c) Is the date correct?

_____

d) Are the actions of the historical figures accurate?

_____

6. As far as you can determine, what are some of the most obvious fictional characters and details of the novel?

_____

_____

_____

_____

_____

Unit: Immigration

Integrated Subject: Social Studies

Assignment

    Using traditional library resources and oral history, the students will research factual information and report on a specific immigrant group to the United States. Each student will prepare a written report and an oral demonstration illustrating a particular facet of the culture.

Library Media Skills
- Introducing techniques for properly interviewing persons to gather data from original sources
- Reviewing the techniques for researching and reporting on a topic

Social Studies Curriculum Content
- Researching the chronology of the arrival of immigrant groups to the United States
- Researching the experience of the immigrant groups
- Investigating immigration legislation
- Exploring the contributions of ethnic groups and individuals to the United States
- Fostering pride in the accomplishments and struggles of the immigrant groups
- Practicing critical thinking

Resources and Materials
- *Makers of America*
- *Encyclopedia of American Ethnic Groups*
- *The American Family Album*
- *Cultures of America*
- *American Immigration*
  http://www.bergen.org/AAST/Projects/Immigration/index.html
- Community resources such as museums and historical societies
- Individuals with first-hand information
- Library resources pertinent to the topic
- Handouts

Activities
1. The teacher presents the assignment, explaining requirements, timeline, and anticipated outcomes.
2. The library teacher reviews notetaking and bibliographic techniques and introduces pertinent library resources.
3. The library teacher shows video of a television interviewer, such as Barbara Walters or Tom Brokaw, and presents methods of interviewing to gather oral history.
4. The students begin research by identifying sources and methods they wish to use in their research.
5. The students complete research, organize information into the report, and prepare demonstration.

Immigration: The Interview Process

Pre-interview Guidelines
* Be prepared before approaching the subject of your interview. Do some background reading so that you will ask intelligent and pertinent questions.
* Prepare a list of questions that will be the framework of the interview.
* Be comfortable in the medium in which you plan to record your interview.
* Introduce yourself and your reason for the interview. Explain why you chose the person to be the subject for your interview.
* Talk about how you plan to record and present the interview (i.e., written report, tape recording, video).
* Be sure to thank the interviewee.

Suggested Questions
* When did you come from (country) and how old were you at the time?
* Did you come alone or with your family?
* What are your memories of the country from which you came?
* Did you bring any memento or tradition that holds special meaning to you and your family?
* How did you get to this country and where did you disembark?
* Tell me something about your journey and arrival in this country.
* How have your experiences met or not met your expectations?
* What are some of the customs from (country) that you still practice?
* America is called the "Great Melting Pot" because it is a mixture of the contributions of many ethnic groups. What do you see as some of the contributions of (country)-Americans?
* Are there any (country)-Americans that you particularly admire?
* Did you ever experience prejudice against you because of your ethnic background? Please tell me what happened and how it made you feel.
* Were you or anyone you know discriminated against when trying to get a job, join a club, or find housing?
* Do you feel this prejudice still exists today?
* What advice would you give a person immigrating to the United States today?

Bibliography for an interview
Fitzmaurice, Mary. Personal interview. 26 August 1995.
Wolfe, Tom. <u>The Wrong Stuff: American Architecture</u>. Videocassette. Dir. Tom Bettag. Carousel Films, 1983.

Unit: Biographical References

Integrated Subject: Social Studies

Assignment

Students will use four specific reference sources to locate information about famous people.

Library Media Skills
- Using four biographical references
- Learning the formats of the references
- Learning the similarities and differences among the four

Social Studies Curriculum Content
- Using four biographical references especially beneficial to the social studies discipline

Resources and Materials
- *Webster's Biographical Dictionary*
- *Current Biography*
- *Dictionary of American Biography*
- *McGraw-Hill Encyclopedia of World Biography*
- Worksheet

Activities
1. The library teacher explains the formats and unique uses of the four biographical references
2. After worksheet and references are distributed, the subject and library teacher circulate to assist individual students.
3. Upon completion of worksheet, answers are discussed and worksheet is collected.

NAME _____ PERIOD _____

DATE _____ **BIOGRAPHICAL REFERENCES**

I. *Webster's Biographical Dictionary*

    A. Who is James Braille Fraser? _____

    B. In what county of Virginia was George Washington born?

    _____

    C. How long is the entry on George Washington? _____

    D. How does this compare to most others in Webster's?

    _____

II. *Current Biography*

    A. What yearbook are you using? _____

    B. Its cumulated index covers 19 ____ to 19 ____ ; this index is located at the

    _____ of the book.

    C. The entries are arranged _____ .

    D. What basic information is given at the beginning of each entry?

    _____

    E. Each entry contains a _____ of the person; the average

    of each article is _____ pages.

    F. One section of the volume you are using has the persons classified by profession. From each of the following categories give the name of one person whose biography is in your book:

    Business_____

    Education _____

    Government _____

Law _____

Literature _____

Military _____

Music _____

Sports _____

III. *Dictionary of American Biography*

    A. What volume are you using? _____

    B. How are the entries arranged? _____

    C. Name one person covered in the volume you are using.

       _____

    D. What contribution to American life did this person make that justifies his /her being

       included in the *DAB*?

       _____

       _____

IV. *McGraw-Hill Encyclopedia of World Biography*

    A. What volume are you using? _____

    B. Choose a person from a country other than the United States.

       _____

    C. How is the person described in the introduction (in colored print) ?

       _____

       _____

    D. How long is the article? _____

    E. What was given at the end of the article? _____

Unit: Civil Rights

Integrated Subject: Social Studies

Assignment

The students each choose from among a large list of suggested topics covering civil rights in its broadest sense—not only the events of the sixties but also situations affecting the lives of several minority groups. After researching the chosen topic and organizing the information, each student writes a paper complete with parenthetical references and bibliography.

Library Media Skills

- Locating appropriate reference materials
- Synthesizing information
- Taking notes
- Writing an organizational plan
- Using parenthetical references
- Writing a bibliography

Social Studies Curriculum Content

- Learning about the civil rights of many minority groups

Suggested Topics

- Topics listed on attached topic sheet

Resources and Materials

- *Great Events*, microfiche produced by the *New York Times*
- *Great Personalities*, microfiche produced by the *New York Times*
- *Eyes on the Prize* (laser disc and videocassette)
- Martin Luther King, Jr.—the Man, the Movement, the Legacy
  http://www.seattletimes.com/mlk/
- Stamp on Black History
  http://library.advanced.org/10320/
- The History Net
  http://www.thehistorynet.com
- Books and nonprint resources on civil rights and minority groups
- Electronic encyclopedias
- Periodicals
- List of suggested topics

Activities

1. The classroom teacher has covered the civil rights movement in class, so students are coming to the project with a base of knowledge about the major developments of

the time period. In this project, they will be researching a specific topic pertinent to the unit and will be asked to draw conclusions based upon their research.

2. The library teacher distributes the project sheet explaining the various choices.
3. The library teacher explains the sources.
4. The students take the remainder of their first period in the library to look at sources and make their choices of topics.
5. On the second day in the library, the library teacher reviews notetaking on cards, techniques for highlighting and writing key words on printouts, and bibliography. The library teacher also calls the students' attention to the information that is necessary for parenthetical references.
6. Students research and take notes on their chosen topics.
7. The library teacher reviews or instructs the students on the proper use of parenthetical references. This is most effectively done when students are near the end of their research time.
8. The library teacher reviews techniques for organizing information.
9. Students write organizational plans and rough drafts.
10. The library teacher and the classroom teacher correct rough drafts.
11. Students revise and write final drafts.

Civil Rights Project: Handout

1. Is forced busing an effective way to integrate schools?

2. How did Rosa Parks make a difference in the civil rights movement?

3. Is the quota system an effective way to end discrimination?

4. Does discrimination exist in professional sports?

5. Is there a connection between racism and poverty?

6. Discuss the changes in the status of minorities in the military since World War I.

7. Has school desegregation made schools equal?

8. Is there a crisis in housing for minority groups?

9. Discuss the role of the Bakke case in the history of discrimination.

10. How has the role of African Americans in politics changed in the last twenty-five years?

11. Why is the achievement of Jesse Owens so remarkable?

12. Why was the KKK formed, and how is it active today?

13. What is the Neo-Nazi movement, and how is it active today?

14. Compare and contrast the organizations that have promoted African-American equality—NAACP, CORE, and SNCC.

15. What has been the plight of Amerasian children since the Vietnam War?

16. What is the glass ceiling, and how does it affect women's opportunities in the workplace?

17. Discuss the work of Cesar Chavez in helping Hispanics.

18. Compare and contrast Japanese-American internment camps and the Nazi concentration camps?

19. What obstacles have Native Americans faced in maintaining their culture and heritage?

20. Why was the achievement of Jim Thorpe so remarkable?

Unit: Colonial Living

Integrated Subject: Social Studies

Assignment

Using library resources, students investigate everyday life in colonial times, select a specific aspect, gather information, and report on that information. Reporting many be done in any medium approved by the teacher or the library teacher.

Library Media Skills
- Learning a variety of reference sources
- Extracting key ideas from many types of sources
- Taking notes on cards
- Writing bibliographic entries from a variety of sources

Social Studies Curriculum Content
- Investigating the daily life of people in colonial times
- Using information to write a report, create a colonial craft, write a skit showing a phase of life, and so on

Suggested Topics

Shopkeeping	Life of a peddler
Colonial crafts	Occupation (i.e., miller, cooper)
Social life	Food and eating habits
Courtship and marriage	Medicine
Education	Religion
Sports	Daily life of a woman
Newspapers	Music
Clothing	Houses and their furnishings

Resources and Materials
- Books on colonial living including:
  Colonial American Living series
  Everyday Things in American Life
  Home Life in Colonial Days
  Home and Child Life in Colonial Days
  Life in Colonial America
  Colonial America
  Colonial Living
- Issues of *Early American Life* magazine
- A Walking Tour of Plimoth Plantation
  http://spirit.lib.uconn.edu/ArchNet/Topical/
- The History Net
  http://www.thehistorynet.com

Activities

1. The classroom teacher introduces the colonial living unit and its significance in the history of the United States.
2. The classroom teacher explains the assignment to the students.
3. The library teacher explains the variety of sources available.
4. The students select topics.
5. The library teacher teaches or reviews notetaking and bibliography.
6. The students complete research and organize information into a report.

Suggestion

This is a perfect time to correlate school activities with the community. Locate individuals in the community who practice colonial crafts or occupations as hobbies or occupations and arrange demonstrations or even a fair. Students could participate in the fair as well.

TECHNOLOGY

Unit: Space Exploration

Integrated Subject: Technology

Assignment

Students will research some important developments in the U.S. space program. Each student will write information on a worksheet and then organize the information on a timeline of these major advances. Finally, each student will locate a picture of a space vehicle, satellite, or other device used in space and construct a model of this item.

Library Media Skills
- Using encyclopedias and almanacs
- Using reference materials in the field of science
- Using on-line resources, if available
- Synthesizing information

Technology Curriculum Content
- Learning about the historical developments in the space program
- Recognizing the progressive development of the space program
- Recognition of current developments in the space program
- Building a model of a vehicle, satellite, or other item necessary to the space program

Resources and Materials
- *Dorling Kindersley Science Encyclopedia*
- *Science and Technology Illustrated*
- *Kingfisher Science Encyclopedia*
- *Growing Up with Science*
- *Life in Space*
- *History of NASA—America's Voyage to the Stars*
- *What Happened When*
- *Famous First Facts*
- *Timeliner*
- NASA Spacelink
  http://spacelink.msfc.nasa.gov
- Hubble Site
  http://quest.arc.nasa.gov/livefrom/hst.html
- Encyclopedias
- Almanacs
- On-line access
- Worksheet

Activities
1. The library teacher introduces the lesson, pointing out resources and passing out the

worksheets. The library teacher and the technology teacher point out that students should recognize the careful planning involved in the space program and the way in which each success is the basis for future work.

2. If available, students use on-line services to locate a current development in the space program.

3. Students complete the worksheet.

4. Students use a computer program such as *Timeliner* to construct a time line of the landmarks of the space program. If no program is available, students write their information on poster board.

5. The technology teacher explains the model that students will be building.

6. Students locate a picture of an object from the space program, such as Mercury, Gemini, or Apollo spacecrafts, lunar rover, space suit, lunar module, space shuttle, or Skylab. Students use the picture as a guide to build a model in technology class.

LANDMARKS OF THE UNITED STATES SPACE PROGRAM

For each of the following important developments in the U.S. space program, write the date of the flight, the name of the vehicle, and the names of the astronauts.

1. First American in space

2. First American in orbit

3. First American walk in space

4. First docking of one American space vehicle with another

5. First American spacecraft to orbit the moon

6. First American landing on the moon

7. First use of a lunar rover

8. First American piloted orbiting space station

9. First flight of a space shuttle

10. Launch of Hubble Telescope

List two other landmarks of the American space program that you would like to include on your time line. Give dates, vehicle names, and names of astronauts.

Locate a site on the Internet that provides information about current developments in the space program. Write the date, project name, and activity that is being engaged in. Include this on your time line.

Landmarks of the United States Space Program—Answer Sheet

1. date: May 5, 1961
   vehicle: Mercury-Redstone 3
   astronaut: Alan B. Shepard, Jr.

2. date: February 20, 1962
   vehicle: Mercury-Atlas 6
   astronaut: John H. Glenn, Jr.

3. date: June 3, 1965-June 7, 1965
   vehicle: Gemini-Titan 4
   astronauts: Edward H. White who walked in space and James A.
      McDivitt

4. date: March 16, 1966-March 17, 1966
   vehicle: Gemini-Titan 8
   astronauts: Neil A. Armstrong and David R. Scott

5. date: May 18, 1969-May 26, 1969
   vehicle: Apollo-Saturn 10
   astronauts: Thomas P. Stafford, John W. Young and Eugene
      Cernan

6. date: July 16, 1969-July 24, 1969
   vehicle: Apollo-Saturn 11
   astronauts: Neil A. Armstrong and Edwin W. Aldrin, Jr., who landed on
   the moon, and Michael Collins

7. date: July 26, 1971-August 7, 1971
   vehicle: Apollo-Saturn 15
   astronauts: David R. Scott, James B. Irwin, and Alfred M. Worden

8. date: May 25, 1973-June 22, 1973
   vehicle: Skylab 2
   astronauts: Charles Conrad, Joseph P. Kerwin, and Paul J. Weitz

9. date: April 12, 1981-April 14, 1981
   vehicle: Columbia
   astronauts: John W. Young and Robert L. Crippen

10. date: April 24, 1990-April 29, 1990
    vehicle: Discovery
    astronauts: Bruce McCandless, Kathryn Sullivan, Loren J. Shriver,
    Charles F. Bolden, Jr., and Steven A. Hawley

Unit: Inventions

Integrated Subject: Technology

Assignment

 Students will gather information and prepare an oral report on an invention including the history and an explanation of how the invention works. Students also create a model of the invention. This will be shown and demonstrated as part of the oral presentation.

Library Media Skills
- Locating information on inventions in print and electronic sources
- Synthesizing information
- Organizing information

Technology Curriculum Content
- Recognizing the progress of technology
- Learning about an invention in historical and technological terms
- Building a model of an invention

Suggested Topics
- Topics listed on attached topic sheet

Resources and Materials
- *The Way Things Work* (book and compact disc)
- *Science and Technology Illustrated*
- *Kingfisher Science Encyclopedia*
- *How It Works*
- *Growing Up with Science*
- *A History of Technology and Invention*
- *Inventors and Discoverers*
- *All about Famous Inventors and Their Inventions*
- *Stories behind Everyday Things*
- *Men of Science and Invention*
- *Discovery by Chance*
- *Inventions that Made History*
- *Eureka!*
- *The Art of Invention*
- *The Scientific Breakthrough*
- *Everyday Inventions*
- *A History of Invention*
- *From Spinning Wheel to Spacecraft*
- *The Smithsonian Book of Invention*
- *Those Inventive Americans*

- *Invention*—Eyewitness Books
- *Inventions-Inventors and Ingenious Ideas*
- *World Book of Great Inventions*
- Encyclopedias (book and compact disc)

Activities

1. The technology teacher introduces the topic of invention and directs student choice of topic.
2. The library teacher introduces sources for research on the history and technology of inventions.
3. Students collect information on the history of their inventions with the assistance of the library teacher and the classroom teacher.
4. The library teacher gives direction on organizing information particularly for an oral presentation.
5. The technology teacher gives instruction on model making.

Inventions: Handout

airplane

automobile

battery

calculator

camera—movie

camera—still

camera—video

cassette player

clock

compact disc player

computer

engine—diesel

engine—gasoline

engine—internal combustion

engine—steam

light bulb

loom

microscope

motor

printing press

radio

refrigerator

sewing machine

spinning wheel

stethoscope

telegraph

telephone

telescope

television

typewriter

vacuum cleaner

Unit: The World of the Future

Integrated Subject: Technology

Assignment

Divided into cooperative learning groups, students will prepare a television news program that could take place in 2050. Their program must include at least the following segments: news, science, the environment, and arts/entertainment. Because the news program will be videotaped, student groups must supply visual support for their stories.

Library Media Skills

- Locating information in print and electronic sources
- Using the Internet for research information
- Notetaking
- Organizing a news program and preparing a story board
- Videotaping a news program

Technology Curriculum Content

- Learning about the current status of technology as it affects our world
- Determining logical trends based on current status particularly in the fields of science and technology
- Creating visual representations to support their news stories on the future

Resources and Materials

- Books
- Periodicals
- Internet
- Electronic encyclopedias
- Videotaping equipment

Activities

1. The classroom teacher and the library teacher introduce the topic emphasizing that developments in all areas of human endeavor are based on what has gone before. Therefore, the projections students make must be logical in terms of what is now.
2. The library teacher explains the use of pertinent sources, including periodical indexes and electronic sources, and provides instruction on developing a story board.
3. Student groups meet to divide responsibilities for research.
4. Students research their topics with the aid of the library teacher and the classroom teacher.
5. Working again in groups, students divide the responsibilities for writing and preparing visual presentations. Students must also prepare any station logos or call letters that they wish to show on the screen.

215

6. Students prepare a story board so the camera person knows who should be on screen.
7. Since all members of the group will participate on camera, camera operation is done by a student from another group with the assistance of the library teacher and the classroom teacher.

Suggestions

This unit may be done in conjunction with the reading of science fiction in English class. Also, if equipment is available, students may prepare a computer presentation instead of a videotaped one.

The World of the Future: Handout

Suggested Topics for News Stories in 2050

Wildlife	Entertainment
World issues	Clothing
Space program	Language
Energy	Housing
Waste salvage	Robotics
Cities	Medicine
Inventions	Communications
Foods	Careers
Education	Transportation
Recreation	Undersea development
Cybernetics	Laser technology
Natural resources	Businesses and industries
Sports	

ADDENDA

Table of Lessons and Library Media Skills Taught

General Lessons

Unit: Orientation—Lesson #1

Learning basic procedures for using the library media center

Learning the location of significant sites in the library media center

Unit: Orientation—Lesson #2

Understanding the different types of searches to be done in a catalog

Using the card catalog or automated catalog to do author, title, and subject searches

Locating materials

Learning about the different types of periodicals subscribed to by the media center and supplying titles for various subject categories

Reviewing or learning to use audiovisual equipment and computers

Unit: Orientation—Lesson #3

Locating information on a given subject in a variety of sources

Using the library catalog

Using encyclopedias

Using magazine indexes, in book and compact disc formats

Using the pamphlet file

Synthesizing facts from a variety of sources

Unit: Orientation—Lesson #4

Learning to use reference materials from different Dewey categories

Synthesizing information

Unit: Orientation—Lesson #5

Learning to find specific information from reference materials

Synthesizing information

Unit: Notetaking

Notetaking using index cards

Reading to extract inportant ideas

Expressing ideas in an original manner

Unit: Bibliography

Identifying the correct components for specific bibliographic entries

Compiling a bibliography using proper components, punctuation, and spacing

Unit: Searching the Internet

>Identifying tools to search the Internet for information
>Using two of these tools, Yahoo and Hot Bot, to search the Internet
>Using Boolean and proximity searching to locate information
>Comparing and contrasting the results

Integrated Subject: Art

Unit: A Historical Perspective on American Architecture

>Finding information in print and nonprint resources
>Synthesizing information

Unit: The Influence of Classical Architecture on Local Buildings

>Finding information in print and electronic sources
>Synthesizing information

Unit: Art History, Art Appreciation

>Selecting appropriate resources for research
>Using research strategies, particular emphasis to be placed on the value of indexes and tables of contents
>Taking notes in a prescribed form
>Organizing information
>Writing a bibliography for all sources according to the prescribed form

Integrated Subject: English

Unit: Magazines

>Reviewing various types of magazines
>Understanding that the mission of a magazine is reflected in its advertising, editorial policy, and content

Unit: Poetic Devices

>Becoming aware of poetry collection
>Understanding of the importance of citing sources, albeit informally

Unit: Mythology

>Checking indexes and tables of contents to identify appropriate sources
>Using illustrations, charts, and maps to locate and sketch major constellations
>Extracting and reporting relevant information
>Compiling a bibliography in correct form

Unit: Folklore

>Locating information in print and nonprint sources

Synthesizing and organizing information

Unit: Favorite Authors

Finding information in print and electronic sources
Synthesizing and taking notes on notecards
Organizing information
Using parenthetical references as necessary
Preparing a bibliography

Unit: African Americans in Arts and Letters

Finding information in print and electronic sources
Synthesizing and organizing information

Unit: Novels—Literary Criticism

Selecting and using biographical references sources
Using cross references
Finding specific sources of information
Practicing and using techniques of notetaking
Selecting and reading a book by the student's chosen author

Integrated Subject: Foreign Language

Unit: Travel Tips

Locating and using reference sources
Synthesizing information and taking notes on cards
Preparing a bibliography

Unit: Current Events in Foreign Countries

Reviewing the use of cross references and key word terms
Using magazine indexes in book and electronic form
Completing a correct bibliography entry for the form used
Skimming an article to locate main and supporting ideas

Integrated Subject: Health

Unit: Disease Research

Identifying and selecting sources relating to the topic
Extracting relevant information
Synthesizing information
Taking and organizing notes using prescribed procedures
Compiling a correct bibliography

Unit: Substance Abuse

       Using magazine and *SIRS* indexes

       Reading articles and synthesizing information

       Compiling a bibliography

Integrated Subject: Home Economics

Unit: *Consumer Reports*

       Using a periodical index

       Learning about the range of products covered and the thoroughness and impartiality
           of *Consumer Reports*

Unit: Career Exploration

       Using "Index by Profession" in the *Current Biography*

       Becoming familiar with the layout of the yearbook and the types of information
           presented in the articles

Unit: Conflict Resolution

       Learning that life lessons are dealt with in fiction and biography

       Selecting a novel or biography that deals with a specific subject

       Reading a novel or biography critically

       Writing about literature

Integrated Subject: Mathematics

Unit: Careers in Mathematics

       Using the library catalog to locate career information

       Learning to use specific career-related materials

Unit: Census

       Using almanacs

       Using the Internet

Integrated Subject: Music

Unit: Composers

       Locating compact discs, cassette tapes, and records of the composer's work

       Locating information on the composer's life, work, and impact

       Scanning for information

       Taking notes

       Compiling a bibliography

Unit: What's That You're Hearing?
        Using indexes effectively
        Becoming familiar with different methods of indexing
        Skimming to locate information
        Choosing main thoughts and supporting details
        Noting sources

Integrated Subject: Physical Education

Unit: The Olympics
        Selecting appropriate materials
        Synthesizing relevant information
        Writing bibliographic entries from various sources

Unit: Sport Investigation
        Locating and using specific reference sources
        Notetaking
        Synthesizing information

Unit: Sports Personalities
        Notetaking from an oral presentation
        Learning about biographical tools in general and the specific purposes and features of
            Current Biography

Integrated Subject: Reading

Unit: Biography Book Talks
        Locating information on inventions in print and electronic sources
        Synthesizing information
        Organizing information

Unit: Readers' Forum
        Furthering an appreciation of reading
        Sharing impressions of reading with peers

Unit: Book Reviews on Disc
        Reading critically
        Selecting details to include in a book review
        Entering data in a database

Integrated Subject: Science

Unit: Classification of Organisms
     Practicing the use of indexes
     Learning the uses and the presentations of several scientific references

Unit: Science in the News
     Skimming to locate information
     Reading carefully to locate facts
     Selecting main thoughts and supporting details

Unit: Chemical Element Report
     Locating and using specific science reference sources
     Using book and electronic indexes with the stress on cross referencing and key word searches
     Compiling a working bibliography

Unit: Biography of a Scientist
     Using the library catalog
     Reading to obtain facts and taking notes on cards
     Synthesizing and paraphrasing information

Unit: Experiment
     Locating and using library resources
     Stating source in correct bibliographic form

Unit: Scientific Classification
     Using library catalog and book indexes

Unit: Physical Science Research
     Locating and using a variety of reference sources
     Selecting and verifying a research topic
     Finding needed information
     Compiling a working bibliography
     Notetaking
     Writing a report including a correct bibliography

Unit: Energy—Critical Thinking
     Locating and selecting appropriate materials
     Using magazine indexes in book and electronic form
     Using *Social Issues and Resources Series* in print and electronic form

Unit: Plant Organism Collection Project

      Locating nature field guides and other pertinent materials by using the library catalog

      Studying illustrations in scientific materials to identify plant organisms

      Compiling a bibliography

Unit: Animal Investigation

      Using library catalog to locate sources

      Using science materials in print and electronic forms

Integrated Subject: Social Studies

Unit: Introduction to Report Writing/Explorers

      Selecting appropriate sources and preparing a working bibliography

      Notetaking in a prescribed manner

      Reading for information

      Synthesizing data and organizing material

      Writing a report including a bibliography

Unit: Social Studies References

      Locating and using specific reference books

Unit: The Forgotten Presidents

      Using specific biographical and historic references to locate information

      Taking effective notes

      Compiling a bibliography of at least two sources

Unit: Historical Fiction

      Identifying the elements of a specific literary genre

      Developing the habit of leisure reading

      Becoming a discriminating reader

      Writing a bibliography

Unit: Immigration

      Introducing techniques for properly interviewing persons to gather data from original sources

      Reviewing the techniques for researching and reporting on a topic

Unit: Biographical References

      Using four biographical references

      Learning the formats of the references

      Learning the similarities and differences among the four

Unit: Civil Rights

Locating appropriate reference materials
Synthesizing information
Taking notes
Writing an organizational plan
Using parenthetical references
Writing a bibliography

Unit: Colonial Living

Learning a variety of reference sources
Extracting key ideas from many types of sources
Taking notes on cards
Writing bibliographic entries from a variety of sources

Integrated Subject: Technology

Unit: Space Exploration

Using encyclopedias and almanacs
Using reference materials in the field of science
Using on-line resources, if available
Synthesizing information

Unit: Inventions

Locating information on inventions in print and electronic sources
Synthesizing information
Organizing information

Unit: The World of the Future

Locating information in print and electronic sources
Using the Internet for research information
Notetaking
Organizing a news program and preparing a story board
Videotaping a news program

References Used

* **000 Generalities**
  SIRS in book and electronic form
  SIRS Digest
  Magazine indexes in book and electronic form
  > *Readers' Guide, Proquest, Primary Search, Middle Search*
  Encyclopedias in book and electronic form
  Periodicals
  > *School Library Journal, Horn Book, Booklist, English Journal, Early American Life, Consumers' Reports*
  Travel periodicals
  Almanacs
  Pamphlet files
  Famous First Facts

* **200 Religion**
  Mythology: An Illustrated Encyclopedia
  A Guide to the Gods
  Illustrated Encyclopedia of Mythology
  New Larousse Encyclopedia of Mythology
  A Companion to World Mythology
  Standard Dictionary of Folklore, Mythology, and Legend
  Redshift2

* **300 Social Sciences**
  Dictionary of Occupational Titles
  Encyclopedia of Careers and Vocational Guidance
  Occupational Handbook
  On-line Career Services

* **500 Pure Science**
  Dorling Kindersley Science Encyclopedia
  Kingfisher Science Encyclopedia
  Growing Up with Science
  North American Wildlife
  Parade of the Animal Kingdom
  International Wildlife Encyclopedia
  Larousse Encyclopedia of Animal Life
  Pictorial Encyclopedia of Insects
  Birds of America
  Imperial Collection of Audubon Animals
  Animal Atlas of the World
  National Geographic Book of Mammals (book and CD)

Macmillan Illustrated Science Encyclopedia
Encyclopedia of Insects
Oxford Book of Invertebrates
Encyclopedia of Reptiles and Amphibians
Animals Without Backbones
Oxford Encyclopedia Trees of the World
Reader's Digest
International Wildlife Encyclopedia
Encyclopedia of Reptiles and Amphibians
Wild Flowers
New Junior Encyclopedia of Science
New Book of Popular Science
Concise Encyclopedia of the Sciences
Harper Encyclopedia of Science
Van Nostrand's Scientific Encyclopedia
Nature Projects for Young Scientists
Background Scientist Series Two and Four
Science Experiments You Can Eat
Science in Your Backyard
Projects in Space Science
Space Projects for Young Scientists
Experimenting with Light
Experiments with Light and Illusions
Investigate and Discover Light
Experiment with Light and Mirrors
Experiments with Motion
Experimenting with Sound
Designs in Science
    Using Light
    Materials Using Sound
    Water
    Using Energy
    Movement
Everyday Material Science Experiments
    Force and Energy
    Air and Gases
    Salts and Solids
    Water and Other Liquids
    Plastics and Polymers
Experimenting with Plants
Experimenting with a Microscope
Exploring with the Microscope
Investigating Nature Through Outdoor Projects
Science Projects about Chemistry
Adventures with Atoms and Molecules

Experimenting with Surface Tension and Bubbles
Astronomy Activity Book
International Wildlife Encyclopedia
Macmillan Illustrated Science Encyclopedia
Encyclopedia of Reptiles and Amphibians
Animal Atlas of the World

* **600 Technology**

The Complete Home Medical Encyclopedia
The Encyclopedia of Health and the Human Body
Family Health and Medical Guide
The Incredible Machine
The Body in Question
The Rand McNally Atlas of the Body and Mind
The Marshall Cavendish Illustrated Encyclopedia of Family Health
Family Doctor (compact disc)
How It Works
The Way Things Work (in book and compact disc form)
Encyclopedia of Science and Technology
The New Book of Popular Science
Life in Space
History of NASA—America's Voyage to the Stars
Science and Technology Illustrated
A History of Technology and Invention
All About Famous Inventors and Their Inventions
Stories Behind Everyday Things
Discovery by Chance
Invention that Made History
Eureka
The Art of Invention
The Scientific Breakthrough
Everyday Inventions
A History of Invention
From Spinning Wheel to Spacecraft
The Smithsonian Book of Invention
Those Inventive Americans Invention —Eyewitness Books
Inventions-Inventors and Ingenious Ideas
World Book of Great Inventions

* **700 The Arts**

Art of Our Century
Art
A Child's History of Art
American Art Now
Fifty Centuries of Art

17th & 18th Century Art
Famous Paintings
Twentieth Century Art
Great Painters
Surrealism
American Painting
Masters of Art
Masterpieces of American Painting
A New World History
A History of Art
American Art of Our Century
Understanding Art
The Story of Art
Pop Art
Your Art Heritage
Impressionism
History of Art
Cubism
Modern Painting
Women Impressionists
The Story of Painting for Young People
Masterpieces of American Painting in the Metropolitan Museum of Art
Larousse Encyclopedia of Modern Art
Great Artists of the Western World Series, 1 & 2
Oxford Companion to Music
International Encyclopedia to Music and Musicians
Oxford Junior Companion to Music
Milton Cross' Encyclopedia of Great Composers and Their Music
Britannia Book of Music
The Buildings of Ancient Egypt
The Romance of Architecture
From Tepees to Towers
The First Book of Architecture
All the Ways of Building
Grand Constructions
City
Encyclopedia of Sports
Rand McNally Encyclopedia of Sports
Official Encyclopedia of Sports
Oxford Companion to World Sports and Games
Great Athletes; The Twentieth Century
Harlem Renaissance

* **800 Literature**
Literary History of the United States

Oxford Companion to English Literature
Oxford Companion to American Literature
Writers' America

* **900   General Geography and History**
Background Notes
World and its People
Culturgrams
Travel guides
Webster's New Geographical Dictionary
The North American Indian
The World of American Indians
Indians of the Longhouse
Webster's Geographical Dictionary
Historical Atlas
Concise Dictionary of American History
Dictionary of American History
The Encyclopedia of American Facts and Dates
Encyclopedia of American History
Colonial American Living series
Everyday Things in American Life
Home Life in Colonial Days
Home and Child Life in Colonial Days
Life in Colonial America
Colonial America
Colonial Living
Chronology of the United States
Makers of America
Encyclopedia of American Ethnic Groups
The American Family Album
Cultures of America
Shepard's Historical Atlas
What Happened When
Great Events, microfiche produced by the *New York Times*
Eyes on the Prize (laser disc and video)

* **920   Biography**
Who's Who in America
Current Biography (book and compact disc form)
Twentieth Century Authors
American Authors 1600-1900
Something About the Author
Authors of Books for Young People
Junior Author Series
Writers for Children

American Authors 1600-1900
British Authors
American Biographies
Major Authors and Illustrators for Children and Young Adults
Speaking for Ourselves, I and II
Authors and Artists for Young Adults
Junior Discovering Authors (compact disc)
McGraw-Hill Encyclopedia of World Biography
Concise Dictionary of American Biography
Webster's American Biography
Webster's Biographical Dictionary
Dictionary of American Biography
Scientists and Inventors
Asimov's Biographical Encyclopedia of Science and Technology
Concise Dictionary of Scientific Biography
Notable American Women
Dictionary of World Biography
The Presidents: a Reference History
Facts about the Presidents
The Glorious Burden
The Complete Book of Presidents
The Discovers
Popular Composers
American Composers Today
Composer Quest on compact disc
Voices of Triumph (VT)
Great Personalities, microfiche produced by the *New York Times*
Inventors and Discoverers

Web Sites

- **General**
  - * Classroom Connect's Citing Internet Resources: A how-to guide for referencing online sources in student bibliography
    http://www.classroom.net/classroom/CitingNetResources.html

- **Art**
  - * Architecture in America (photos)
    http://lcweb2loc.gov/detroit/archamer.html
  - * Architecture through the Ages
    http://library.advanced.org/10098/
  - * Greek Architecture
    http://chs-web.neb.net/usr/katelevy/greek/greek.html
  - * WebMuseum network
    http://sunsite.unc.edu/louvre/
  - * Yahoo's list of artists
    http://www.yahoo.com/Arts/Art_History/Artists/

- **English**
  - * An Index of Poem Titles
    http://library.utoronto.ca/www/utel/rp/indextitles.html
  - * Project Bartleby
    http://columbia.edu/acis/bartleby/index.html
  - * Encyclopedia Mythica
    http://www.pantheon.org/mythica/
  - * The Night Sky/Topical Index of Gods and Goddesses
    http://www.windows.umich.edu/the_universe/constellations.html
  - * Yahoo's Author's List: Fiction
    http://www.yahoo.com/Arts/Humanities/LiteratureGenres/Children_s/Authors/
  - * Yahoo's Author list: Children's
    http://www.yahoo.com/Arts/Humanities/Literature/Genres/Children_s/Authors/
  - * Children's Literature Web Guide: Authors on the Web
    http://www.acs.ucalgary.ca/~dkbrown/authors.html
  - * NBC's Club Noir
    http://www.nbc.com/clubnoir/
  - * Washington Post Book World
    http://www.washingtonpost.com/wp-srv/WPlate/m-bookworld.html
  - * Bookwire Reviews
    http://www.bookwire.com/reviews/
  - * The Hungry Mind Review
    http://www.bookwire.com/hmr/

* The New York Times Book Review
  http://www.nytimes.com/books/
* Carol Hurst's Children's Literature Site
  http://www.carolhurst.com/
* Kiddie Lit on the Net
  http://www.kn.pacbell.com/wired/KidLit/Kid.ht

- **Foreign Language**
  * Yahoo's Countries list
    http://www.yahoo.com/Regional/Countries/
  * U.S. Department of State Background Notes
    http://www.state.gov/www/background_notes/index.html
  * Library of Congress country studies
    http://lcweb2.loc.gov/frd/cs/cshome.html
  * Microsoft Expedia
    http://expedia.msn.com/daily/home/default.hts
  * Africa Guide
    http://www.sas.upenn.edu/Africa_Studies/Home-Page/AFR_GIDE.html
  * Latin American Studies
    http://lanic.utexas.edu/las.html
  * Yahoo International Headlines
    http://yahoo.com/headlines/international/

- **Health**
  * Diseases, Disorders and Related Topics
    http://www.mic.ki.se/Diseases/index.html
  * MedincineNet
    http://www.medicinenet.com/
  * Yahoo's list of Diseases and Conditions
    http://www.yahoo.com/Health/Diseases_and_Conditions/
  * Mayo Clinic Health Oasis
    http://www.mayohealth.org
  * Centers for Disease Control
    http://www.cdc.gov/diseases/diseases.html
  * Partnership for a Drug-Free America
    http://www.drugfreeamerica.org/
  * Web of Addictions
    http://www.well.com/user/woa/
  * Addiction Research Foundation
    http://www.arf.org/isd/info.html

- **Mathematics**
  * Occupational Outlook Handbook
    http://stats.bls.gov/ocohome.htm

* U.S. Bureau of the Census
  http://www.census.gov/

- **Music**
  * Classical Composer Biographies
    http://www.cl.cam.ac.uk/users/mn200/music/composers.html
  * WWW Virtual Library Classical Music page
    http://www.gprep.pvt.k12.md.us/classical/index1.html

- **Physical Education**
  * Yahoo's Olympic Links
    http://www.yahoo.com/Recreation/Sports/Events/International_Games/
    Olympic_Games/
  * Yahoo's list of sports
    http://www.yahoo.com/Recreation/Sports/

- **Science**
  * Science Daily
    http://www.sciencedaily.com/
  * Science News Online
    http://www.sciencenews.org/
  * Discover magazine
    http://www.enews.com/magazines/discover/
  * CNN Sci-Tech
    http://www.cnn.com/TECH/
  * ABCNEWS.com Science
    http://www.abcnews.com/sections/science/index.html
  * Web Elements
    http://www.shef.ac.uk/uni/academic/A-C/chem/web-elements/web-elements
    -home.html
  * Chemicool Periodic Table
    http://the-tech.mit.edu/Chemicool/
  * Web Elements
    http://chemserv.bc.edu/web-elements-home.html
  * Yahoo's List of Scientists
    http://www.yahoo.com/Arts/Humanities/History/Science_and_Technology/
    People/
  * Nobel Prize Internet Archive
    http://www.almaz.com/nobel/
  * 4000 Year of Women in Science
    http://crux.astr.ua.edu/4000WS/4000WS.html
  * Treasure Trove of Scientific Biography
    http://www.astro.virginia.edu/~eww6n/bios/bios.html
  * MacTutor History of Mathematics — Index of Biographies
    http://www.groups.mcs.st-and.ac.uk/~history/BioIndex.html

* The Science Club
  http://www.halcyon.com/sciclub/
* Newton's Apple
  http://ericir.syr.edu/Projects/Newton/
* Franklin Institute
  http://sln.fi.edu/qanda/spotlight1/spotlight1.html
* Animal Bytes Database
  http://seaworld/animal_bytes
* Plant Encyclopedia
  http://www.gardening.com/Encyclopedia/Default.htm
* Botany Classification
  http://www.mancol.edu/science/biology/plants_new/intro.pintlist.html

- **Social Studies**
  * Grolier Online's The American Presidency
    http://www.grolier.com/presidents/preshome.html
  * The President of the United States from The White House
    http://www1.whitehouse.gov/WH/glimpse/presidents/html/presidents.html
  * Internet Public Library's POTUS
    http://www.ipl.org/ref/POTUS
  * Yahoo's List of Presidents
    http://www.yahoo.com/Arts/Humanities/History/U_S__History/People/
    Presidents/
  * American Immigration
    http://www.bergen.org/AAST/Projects/Immigration/index.html
  * Martin Luther King Jr. — the Man, the Movement, the Legacy
    http://www.seattletimes.com/mlk/
  * Stamp on Black History — biographical sketches of past leaders
    http://library.advanced.org/10320/
  * The History Net
    http://www.thehistorynet.com
  * A Walking Tour of Plimouth Plantation
    http://spirit.lib.uconn.edu/ArchNet/Topical

- **Technology**
  * Yahoo's space link
    http://yahoo.com/Science/Space
  * NASA Spacelink
    Spacelink.msfc.nasa.gov
  * Hubble Site
    http://quest.arc.nasa.gov/livefrom/hst/html

About the Authors

Rosann Jweid (BS, SUNY-Oswego; MLS, SUNY-Albany) has worked in both elementary and secondary education. After several years as a classroom teacher, she entered the library field where she spent twenty-five years as a high school and then junior high school librarian. For ten years of this time she was also the Library Department head for her school district. She is currently a library consultant.

Margaret Rizzo (BA, College of Saint Rose; MA, Siena College; MLS, SUNY-Albany) began her career as a high school English teacher and for twenty-five years has been a school library media specialist in a suburban middle school. She also teaches composition and literature at a local community college.